Risk Less and Prosper

Risk Less and Prosper

YOUR GUIDE TO SAFER INVESTING

Zvi Bodie
and
Rachelle Taqqu

WILEY

John Wiley & Sons, Inc.

Published by John Wiley & Sons, Inc., Hoboken, New Jersey.
Published simultaneously in Canada.

For general information on our other products and services or for technical support, please contact our Customer Care Department within the United States at (800) 762-2974, outside the United States at (317) 572-3993, or fax (317) 572-4002.

Wiley also publishes its books in a variety of electronic formats. Some content that appears in print may not be available in electronic books. For more information about Wiley products, visit our web site at www.wiley.com.

Library of Congress Cataloging-in-Publication Data:
Bodie, Zvi.
   Risk less and prosper : your guide to safer investing / Zvi Bodie, Rachelle Taqqu. – 1
      p. cm.
   Includes index.
   ISBN 978-1-118-01430-1 (hardback); ISBN 978-1-118-20623-2 (ebk);
   ISBN 978-1-118-20624-9 (ebk); ISBN 978-1-118-20625-6 (ebk)
      1. Investments.   2. Risk.   3. Finance, Personal.   I. Taqqu, Rachelle, 1947- H. Title.
   HG4521.B5643 2011
   332.024—dc23

                                                                    2011035470

Printed in the United States of America
10 9 8 7 6 5 4 3 2 1

For my grandchildren, my most precious assets

—ZB

For Yael and Jonathan

—RT

Contents

Foreword

The arrival of *Risk Less and Prosper,* with its innovative perspective on how households can take charge of their essential financial decisions involving life-cycle saving and investment, could not have been better timed. These are difficult decisions in difficult times, surrounded by considerable uncertainty involving where we might be, what we might want, and the state of the economic environment, often decades into the future. We are amid a perplexing financial and economic crisis affecting most of the Western world, which further amplifies the uncertainty. How it will play out in the impending future, we do not know. But what we do know is that it is critically important to take charge of one's financial affairs now.

Even before the current crisis, as a result of major technological innovation and widespread deregulation, households have been called on to make a wide range of important and detailed financial decisions that they did not have to in the past. For instance, there is a widespread trend away from defined-benefit pension plans that require no management decisions by the employee toward defined-contribution plans that very much do. In the United States alone, there are more than 8,000 mutual funds and a vast array of other retail investment products to choose from. Along with insurance products and liquidity services, the household thus faces a daunting task to assemble these various components into a coherent effective lifetime financial plan and then implement it.

Some see this trend continuing and widening. Perhaps so, especially in the more immediate future, with the widespread growth of relatively inexpensive Internet access to financial "advice engines" to assist households with financial decisions. However, the creation of all these alternative investment products combined with financial advice offered from so many different sources has consequences: Households have been left with the responsibility for making important and technically complex microfinancial decisions involving risk—decisions that they did not have to make *in the past*, they are not trained to make *in the present*, and they are not likely to execute efficiently *in the future*, even with attempts at education. Financial planners, corporate pension-plan sponsors, and independent pension funds can be helpful, but still the complexity for the individual can be overwhelming.

This book offers a clear, foundational, analytical framework that explains how to go about determining the financial goals you want to achieve; creating a realistic plan to achieve those goals; and then implementing that plan. Writing in plain, jargon-free language, the authors patiently develop their theme and thesis that properly measuring and managing risk of well-specified goals is the foundation for good investment decisions, and they develop guiding principles to do so, based on finance science and informed by practical experience. These principles are applied to develop a risk-management strategy for investment success defined by achievement of goals and to help you avoid paths of error by exposing the flaws of frequently heard, but erroneous, investment rules.

You could not do better than have the Bodie-Taqqu team as your guides. A professor of finance at Boston University for more than 35 years, Zvi Bodie is a premier scientific researcher on retirement finance and investing, particularly on the risk of inflation and the incorporation of human capital into the investment optimization process. He has long been dedicated to creating financial literacy and is the coauthor of a best-selling investment textbook, now in its 9th edition. Rachelle Taqqu is a financial consultant practitioner who, like Bodie, is committed to improving financial decision making for households. She brings hands-on experience of working with individuals on setting and executing their financial course.

The book employs a clever and effective pedagogical approach by creating a story about a group of people with a common need to make financial decisions, who meet to discuss their individual challenges and opportunities with the idea of learning from one another's knowledge and experiences. Although the group and its leader are hypothetical, their characters and challenges are composites drawn from real people and carefully crafted to illustrate a wide range of situations. Through the interactions among the characters, you come to recognize interests, types, and issues in common, and in that way feel a sense of active participation as a virtual member of the group. The journey of the group from knowing little about financial planning and feeling overwhelmed to learning how to execute a well crafted custom-fit plan, including how to select an advisor to help, is presented in three parts.

Part I is all about you, focusing on unlearning ineffective habits from the past and learning a better way to determine a feasible and desirable life-cycle financial plan tailored to you. The process starts with setting financial goals, determining what the risks are that they may not be achieved, and then cycling back to modify those goals until a combination of goals and the risk of not achieving them reaches a comfortable balance. This is undertaken in six steps: (1) Set the goals, (2) know how to monitor progress toward the goals, (3) establish a priority list for the goals, (4) create a time line for achieving those goals, (5) consult with others whose life plans will be directly affected by your plan, and (6) determine what the cost is to achieve those goals. From this, we learn how to create a lifetime budget and convert a dream into a concrete plan.

Part II is dedicated to understanding the critical element of risk in financial decision making. Chapter 4 covers the most commonly encountered fallacies about measuring risk and investing. Chapter 5 takes you through the common psychological mistakes humans make in making decisions under uncertainty. These important and challenging subjects are explained in an intuitive fashion so that you can both understand the fallacies and cognitive errors and become sensitized to recognize them when they are experienced.

The central message is clear: You may easily get less than you pay for, measured either in terms of money or risk protection, but you rarely, if ever, will get more. If it seems too good to be true, it is almost surely not true. There is no free lunch, and if you seem to be offered one, check again—you have probably missed some cost. All important financial decisions involve making trade-offs between what we desire and what we must give up to get it. So if you want a higher-priced lifestyle in retirement, then there are only three ways to improve the chances of getting it: Save more (and consume less) now, work longer (retire later), or take more risk (and accept a larger loss in the event that you do not succeed).

Armed with this sound preparation, Chapter 6 leads you affirmatively through the process of creating a personal risk profile. From all of this emerges a lifetime financial plan framed in reality and specificity with an explicit recognition of the balance between the desired goals and the risks of not achieving them. The process is thus structured to accommodate unpredictable change as one goes through life and the future unfolds into the present.

Part III addresses the implementation of the lifetime plan with ample detail and description of the various financial instruments that can be used to go after the desired goals within the accepted risk profile. Featured are the role of annuities in the retirement part of the life cycle and specialized tax-efficient plans for saving for children's education or for accumulating resources for retirement. You receive a primer on the tools for protecting against the risk of inflation, interest rate risk, and mortality and longevity risks. There is a chapter devoted to risky investing in equities and other asset classes.

Although the book prepares you for financial decision making and implementation, determining a plan and investing to implement it is time consuming and often complicated. Many readers will thus decide that it makes sense to hire a professional, an advisor, to manage and implement their financial plan. Building on the foundation of the preceding chapters, the concluding Chapter 11 takes you through the process, step by step and thoroughly, beginning with helping you determine if you need an advisor, and if you do, then how systematically to go about selecting one.

Risk Less and Prosper is an accessible, bold, and largely self-contained offering of the principles and steps of implementation to achieve your lifetime financial goals, and to better understand, measure, and manage risk in the evolving financial system. Whether you're a first-time investor, a seasoned financial advisor, or a regulator of retail financial services, you are in for a treat: *Bon Appétit!*

ROBERT C. MERTON
MIT, Sloan School of Management

Preface

Something has gone terribly wrong with the way we think about personal investing. Trustworthy investment advice for individuals is hard to find. Much of what goes for advice is filled with misleading promotions masquerading as education, and the result has been pervasive misinformation. Investors are not aware of how much risk they are bearing. Two stock market collapses in seven years have made these failings all too clear.

What's needed is a better investment path—one that leads investors to their financial goals without risking calamity.

This mission has become all the more pressing following the financial earthquake that began in the fall of 2008. Few people have fared well and markets remain volatile. The phasing out of company-sponsored pension plans darkens the picture. Without an employer's pension to rely on, most individuals are left to manage their investments on their own—for retirement and more. When they do look to a trusted advisor for help, it's still the ordinary investor's responsibility to find and pay for such counsel. If individuals and families are to shoulder such a large responsibility, they'll need to be better prepared.

There is an urgent need for impartial advice to combat the confusion and false impressions fostered in much of conventional wisdom. For coauthor Zvi Bodie, this has been a long-term project. He has been an outspoken advocate for educating individuals on the basics and has repeatedly voiced distress at the misconceptions that continue to take investors in. Even in his classes at Boston University's School of Management, where he is the Adele Baron Professor of

Finance, Zvi has encountered confusion from students who should know better but have been influenced more by the industry than the science.

Zvi has been a longtime proponent of integrating insurance perspectives into investment planning. He has persistently emphasized the need to assure yourself a minimum basic income that is safe—whether for retirement, for higher education, or for other long-term goals. Zvi teamed up with coauthor Rachelle Taqqu after they discovered their shared commitment to investor education. As a financial consultant, Rachelle had come across a daunting level of needless mystification in the general public about all things financial, even among the highly educated, and had become an advocate for improving investment literacy.

Over the years, Zvi has seen a growing circle of planners and advisors adopt the core principles of safety-first investing. They too are looking for a source that sets out the safety-first approach in one place—starting from how to think about it and including details about how to get it done.

Risk Less and Prosper has been written for readers at all levels and is targeted especially at the middle class. For the novice, it aims for clarity and simplicity. It's designed to prepare you for action while avoiding harm. And seasoned investors will find a new, across-the-board approach to risk and reward that changes the game for good. But be forewarned: We will be discrediting many chestnuts from the conventional wisdom along the way as we point the direction to a safer alternative.

Setting Goals to Manage Risk

As you read on, you'll be introduced to a small group of men and women who are meeting together, along with a financial advisor, in order to get better at taking charge of their personal investments. All the members of this group are based on composites of real people. All are well educated, except that they're unversed in the basics of finance and investing.

Here is a preview of the fundamentals we'll be covering along with the group.

First and foremost, personal investing is about you—your goals, your values, your career path, and your preferences. In very large measure, it is your goals that drive your investment decisions.

So the safety-first approach you'll read about here also calls for goal-based investing. It encourages you to picture your destinations as clearly as you can. And this is where the book begins.

Your next step is to estimate the price tag of your vision. To decide how much of your vision you need to keep safe, try paring your goals down to the bare essentials. Imagine the minimum you will absolutely need.

How easy is it to come up with answers? Does the picture of your destination come readily to mind? If it does, you are among the lucky ones. Research shows that relatively few people get as far as making a plan, even a very approximate one. This is one of the most common causes of failure—so, if you don't have your destination clearly in mind yet, keep working on it, even if you think your long-term goals are just too far in the future to capture. We'll be looking at ways to help you get a better grasp of both your goals and the investments you'll need to fund them.

It's also important to complete a budgeting drill. Check how well your goals align with the lifetime income you are expecting. Most of the money to meet your goals will probably come from income from your work. This explains why your chosen career path is an important factor in your investment decisions. Of course, you can't predict your route with certainty, but the source and the extent of your income expectations play a key role in setting your investment course.

The exercise of setting goals and aligning them with expected funding sources has a crucial by-product: It helps you decide on the right amount of risk to take. We'll get to the mechanics later on, but the central insight is simple. Setting goals—and quantifying them—clarifies where to draw the line on risk. By establishing the minimal needs that you can't do without, you're also specifying what you cannot afford to lose or risk.

This perspective breaks with convention because it measures risk in terms of possible shortfall *amounts*, and not the *odds* of falling short. So: if you hear the catchphrase that an investment portfolio has a 90 percent chance of getting you to your goal, remember to flip the statement on its head. Ask *how much* you stand to *lose*. Then weigh the consequences.

Because individuals do such a bad job of assessing risk—and because investment risk is so often and so deceptively promoted as a necessity—we'll also spend time surveying the landscape of investment risk. In Part II, we'll look at the ways that risk has been sold to consumers. We'll show how to spot trickery, and how to reframe the questions more honestly.

The ability to take risk is a highly individual matter. It is affected by many factors—including how near or far you are from achieving your financial targets, how much time remains before you need to retire, how reliable your income from work is, and how stable your life circumstances are, among other things.

Stability in work and life circumstances is not always predictable, but you can detect broad outlines. In work, look at the stability of the industry you are in as well as your own position. Life circumstances include your dependents and your marital status, for example, and perhaps your health.

All these factors influence your objective capacity for risk. On the other hand, there is also the matter of how you feel about risk—or your risk tolerance. Having a high subjective tolerance for investment risk is not the same as having a large objective capacity for risk.

Your personal inclination to take investment risk is not easy to gauge. It has nothing to do with your strong attraction to skydiving out of airplanes. But, if you try imagining actual scenarios of loss and gain to test how you'd feel, you may learn something about it.

You may decide, though, that your risk tolerance is not a permanent trait after all, but a passing state that changes with circumstances. If so, you won't pay much attention to it. At the end of Part II, you'll find guidance on how to think about risk tolerance, so you can draw your own conclusions. You'll see why—contrary to conventional wisdom—risk tolerance is only a secondary consideration when you are choosing your investments.

All these notions—matching investments to goals, estimating the level and riskiness of your future earnings, and risk tolerance—will come into play as you chart your individual line of defense against loss. This is the line that determines the right blend of risk and safety for you. Depending on who you are, you may find that the portion of your investments you need to invest safely seems overwhelmingly large. That's not unusual, especially as you approach retirement. In fact, as we'll see, one good way to ensure that you have indeed arrived at the right decision is to start out by hypothetically loading absolutely everything into the safe side, then determine how far that will take you and fine-tune as needed. In any event, remember that you'll surely be making adjustments in future years as you monitor your original investment map to stay up-to-date.

Creating a Safety-First Portfolio

It's often argued that risk-free instruments such as government bonds are not really risk free because you remain exposed to inflation when you own them. We've encountered such claims even from supposedly trustworthy sources, including the web site of the Financial Services Industry Regulatory Agency (FINRA). This argument is *only* correct if you're referring to insured Certificates of Deposit from banks or conventional U.S. Treasury bonds.

But it's a position that's been trumped since 1997, when the U.S. Treasury began issuing Treasury Inflation Protected Securities (TIPS for short), which offer returns that have been adjusted for inflation. There is also a U.S. savings bond called an I Bond, which has different mechanics but also offers a return that keeps holders even with inflation.

When you own TIPS and I Bonds, your initial investment is guaranteed and your return is paid in inflation-adjusted dollars. TIPS are offered in a variety of maturities, so it's possible to build a ladder made up of bonds that mature one after the other. You can readily see how well such an investment lends itself to goal matching. We'll explore the ins and outs of the implementation strategy in a later chapter. For safety and protection against inflation, TIPS and I Bonds are unsurpassed.

It's important to be clear about what's meant by "safety," because nothing is absolutely safe. Life happens; unexpected things occur. And we are living in turbulent times. Nevertheless, just because nothing is completely safe does not mean that everything is equally unsafe.

So, when we look for safe investments, we are looking for the safest investments available. In an era when even strong sovereign credits are being questioned, TIPS and I Bonds are still the safest investments around—especially for individuals who expect to be paying their expenses in U.S. dollars.

In Part III, we'll take you through the ins and outs of TIPS and I Bonds. There are also some other relatively safe products that can be used to serve special purposes. Some states offer educational savings accounts for prepaying college tuition. Insurance companies sell annuities to protect retirees against fluctuating income after they have stopped working. And so on. We'll look at these too as we consider how to build a safety-first, goal-based investment portfolio.

The risky portion of your portfolio comes next. We'll give you a bird's-eye picture of the landscape here, focusing on stocks. We'll include principles to follow, significant traps to watch out for, and how to think about your risky portfolio in general. And finally, we'll give you some essential pointers on how to find an impartial, trustworthy financial advisor.

At no time will we argue that your risk in the stock market goes away or even diminishes over time. This popular and rather seductive belief is a fabrication based on misconception, illusion, and confusion.

Stocks generally have higher returns than lower-risk investments. The premium compensates you for taking risk. There is nothing that magically happens over time to remove the risk from the picture. After you read this book, we expect you to abandon forever the myth that risk in the stock market vanishes or shrinks in the long run.

Of course, if you've created a solid basic layer of safe investments, you'll have the luxury of peace of mind. You can hope for some upside from your risky portfolio with the knowledge that you've created a safety net for yourself in case your stock holdings move against you.

More Science, Less Junk

Goal-based investing is not a passing fad or fancy. It's grounded in science, and its main scientific mooring is in life-cycle economics. By looking at your goals first, we take a page from the life-cycle economist's book, which views your consumption of goods and leisure rather than wealth as the best measure of your financial well-being.

When you calculate how to fund your future goals, you are effectively planning to reduce consumption today in order to spend tomorrow, just as life-cycle economics predicts you will. When you judge success by your ability to meet these goals—rather than by your record in beating some market benchmark—you are also following precepts from economics.

Life-cycle economics further considers your *earning power* (called "human capital" by economists) as a key determinant of both your lifetime income and your wealth. Your total wealth is the sum of your financial wealth and your earnings potential. From this standpoint, it's easy to understand why it's prudent to coordinate your overall investment risk with the risk and reward you expect from your career. If you leave your earning power out of the equation, you can end up with an imbalanced investment strategy that takes either too much or too little risk.

In its focus on life-cycle economics, goal-based investing accords with the centrality of individuals and households to the whole discipline of economics. It's also intuitive—and not just theoretically sound—to use individual goals to define risk and guide personal investing. But this has not been the approach of most conventional personal investing advice.

Instead, personal investing has traditionally focused on the statistical concepts of mean and standard deviation. It relies principally on diversification to manage risk. And it defines risk as volatility, not as the chance of missing your own goals. It looks a lot like a scaled-back version of the institutional playbook.

What's been lost is an appreciation of the unique needs of individuals. Our lives are finite. Sooner or later, we all die. We need to protect ourselves against the consequences of disability, illness, and joblessness, to name just a few. And we need to have our money when we need it. Investment shortfalls can be calamitous.

Institutions, by contrast, face different kinds of risks than individuals do—including competition and price and production risks. It is therefore no surprise that they have developed investment and risk management practices that differ from the practices that best suit individuals. Ultimately, of course, the risks institutions take are borne by the people for whom they exist, and there is plenty of room for overlap between institutional and personal investing. But more attention must be paid to the personal concerns of individuals and families.

This brief survey helps explain the robustness of goal-based investing as a new approach to personal finance. Revision is overdue. It's time to put the individual at the center of the game.

Keeping Things Simple

By asking you to start with yourself and to inventory your goals, we've removed a great deal of clutter. Gone are the endless menu options and the long lists of products to consider. We've banished the prospectuses, the stock ticker, and the breaking news, at least for now. None of the selections on the standard investor menu can make much sense until you set your destination and gauge how you will find the fuel to get there.

Even then, we're going to ask you to stay patient and try to picture what your journey might look like if you decided, say, to set a guaranteed minimum annual income in retirement to cover your essential needs. How much would you have to save? For how long?

You'll probably find that you can progress much faster on this well-defined but minimalist path than you could before. It's critical to keep your options narrow at the beginning, because there is such a thing as too much choice.

Columbia Business School professor Sheena Iyengar demonstrated this in a memorable way in some experiments with exotic jams. In a high-end food market, Iyengar compared the behavior of two groups of shoppers: one group was offered a free taste of as many as 24 fancy jams, the other just six. The results were surprising. The larger display of jams consistently attracted bigger crowds. But the greater attraction did not translate into more sales. After sampling the jams, the customers who'd been offered more limited choices were about *10 times* more likely to actually buy jam.

Separately, Iyengar also looked at how choice affected participation in employer-sponsored retirement plans. She found that adding options caused participation rates to fall. Too much choice has hurt rather than helped investor education.[1]

Keeping it simple is our plan. We'll aim first to build a strong foundation of understanding, and only then delve into the details of investment choices. At each level, the focus will be on you—and on achieving your goals by investing with less risk.

For lots of extra e-freebies related to our book, visit the Companion web site http://risklessandprosper.com.

Acknowledgments

Many people helped in the creation of this book. We are grateful to the members of the Life Cycle Financial Planning and Investing Group for their continuing inspiration: David Griswold, Paula Hogan, Rick Miller, Robert Powell, Kent Smetters, and Karen Maloney Stifler. Additional thanks go to Paula Hogan, Kent Smetters, and Robert Kirchner, who made time to read early chapter drafts and offered valuable suggestions.

Jonathan Treussard, Sundar Srinivasan, Stacy Schaus, Yael Taqqu, Jonathan Taqqu, Eunice Harps, Herb Dreyer, Carol Wool, and Jeremy Levine gave us first-class ideas and feedback. It goes without saying, though, that all mistakes and fumbles are our responsibility alone.

We also appreciate the good guidance and assistance we have received from our team at Wiley: Tiffany Charbonier, Bill Falloon, Meg Freeborn, Sharon Polese, and Pamela van Giessen.

Last but not least, for their patience and loving support, we extend heartfelt thanks to Judy Bodie, Lara Bodie, Moriya Bodie Treussard, and Murad Taqqu.

PART I

ALL ABOUT YOU

CHAPTER 1

Changing the Game

Science is a long history of learning not to fool ourselves.
—Richard Feynman

Not long ago, a woman we know came into some money. It was a substantial but not a breathtaking sum that had come quite unexpectedly from a childless aunt. Julia, as we'll call her, is a diligent, responsible person; and to her surprise and consternation, the inheritance threw her into turmoil for a long time. She had absolutely no idea what to do with the money.

Julia wanted to consult with a financial advisor, but she felt lost when it came to finding one. Although she owned her own business and considered herself financially literate, the prospect of choosing a trustworthy advisor seemed overwhelming to her. Her aunt's attorneys were no help. They were out of state and had no local names to recommend.

Julia began canvassing a few of her friends for advice. She hoped they could share insights, opinions, and with luck, some good referrals, too. She started with Sue, whom she saw often because their children were classmates. She also spoke with Sam, another friend, who worked in her office building. Sam always seemed to be in the know about the latest new thing.

Things did not go as Julia had planned. Instead of generating some interesting but very casual conversations, she found that she'd ignited a fire.

She'd caught Sue just as Sue was trying to learn more about her family's investments. They'd lost what felt like a vast amount during the financial collapse at the end of 2008. Sue was horrified and wondered whether her husband hadn't been playing a little too fast and loose with their money. Until then, he'd assumed sole responsibility for their investments, but Sue was divorcing now and needed to take charge. Just how she would manage to do this she did not know.

Sam, too, responded with unforeseen enthusiasm. Through the accountant who did his taxes, he had just learned of a financial planner—we'll call him Paul—who was hoping to launch a guidance group. He was modeling his group on the support groups he'd been hearing about—people who got together every month or so to help one another learn more about money and investing.

Paul thought a support group could be more motivating and interesting than a classroom could ever be. The groups that had inspired him were not conventional investment clubs or counseling groups to help with budgeting and the like. Rather, what they offered was more like an amalgam of investment education, inspiration, and mutual encouragement.

Paul was peeved that many people seemed to be flying completely blind. They were subjecting themselves to all kinds of misinformation culled from a potpourri of unvetted sources in the library, the Internet, the popular press, television—you name it.

That's how Paul came to hatch a new plan. He was still in the early days of his project when he shared his thoughts with Sam's accountant, who loved the idea and promised to spread the word.

It wasn't long before Sam contacted Paul. He brought Julia and Sue to a meeting—and the three of them liked what they heard. There was a small fee, but the arrangement seemed reasonable to them all.

Paul asked them to recruit one other person, or couple, so they could broaden the experiences they'd be able to talk about. He insisted that they choose someone at a different stage of life, though. The three of them were in their thirties through their late forties, and Paul believed that it would be helpful to include someone in the group who was closer to retirement. It would give them a glimpse of themselves in 15 or 20 years. And the newcomers would benefit too. They'd get a wider view of their options along with the energy of this spirited group.

With the group's blessing, Julia approached an older friend at her health club. They'd bantered together for years at the gym, and Julia thought he, and possibly his wife, might be interested in joining their group. Julia's instinct proved right. Patrick, age 57, and his wife Marianne, 55, were immediately attracted to the proposal. They, too, had suffered big losses in 2008, wanted to get their investments back in shape, but felt vulnerable. Patrick told Julia that the idea was just the ticket he'd been looking for. He didn't know Paul, but he considered the group a low-risk way to learn a lot and to get back on track—all in a friendly, interesting setting.

At their first meeting, knowing that it would be important for their success to identify what they had in common, Paul asked each of them why they'd come. As each took the floor to answer, the others found themselves nodding in agreement as they heard the same feelings of frustration, confusion, and vulnerability repeated again and again.

Julia and Sam were the ones who considered themselves knowledgeable about money and investing, yet both felt either paralyzed or completely flummoxed. They'd both done all the "right" things: They'd saved the maximum amounts allowed in their retirement plans, they'd been disciplined about saving as much as possible, they'd each "diversified" their investments and put 65 to 70 percent in equities as they'd been educated to do, but they had little to show for their effort.

The recent near collapse of the financial markets had paralyzed Julia. She knew she ought to be investing her inheritance, but she was too overwhelmed, intimidated, and confused to make a plan. In addition, she found herself in resistance mode quite often these days. Early on, her two brothers, who had also received shares of the bequest, had been pressuring Julia to join with them in a real estate investment. Julia had refused; it had never felt right to her, and they all now believed they had dodged some bullets. Still, she felt no closer to a solution although some time had already passed.

Sam believed he had a newly clean slate. He was a marketing professional who'd just moved into town from another state after 9 months of unemployment. After working for many years in a much larger firm, he had taken a position in a small technology company. Sam felt chastened about the way he'd handled his money—he'd either spent or lost a big share of his portfolio during his job search. He told the group that he was motivated to do it right this time around, but he still did not know what "right" was.

Sue, a physician with three children, told them how frightening she had found the market's descent and said she wanted to learn more about how to manage risk. But she agreed with the others about how hard it was for her to gain any sense of mastery or control. This she found enormously frustrating. She had developed a pattern of letting herself grow discouraged.

Patrick enjoyed watching the financial news on cable TV and had spent a lot of time researching and trading stocks. But now he was motivated by fear. Both he and his wife Marianne felt lucky to be employed, though the retirement clock preoccupied them and made them both uneasy.

The evening flew by. Paul was excited by what he had started, and they were all surprised by how alike they sounded despite their different circumstances. They enthusiastically scheduled a series of monthly meetings. As an antidote to their shared state of inadequacy and confusion, Paul decided to assign them some things to read, including a few of the best investment web sites geared for people like them.

New Rules

This book has been written as a kind of syllabus for Paul to follow. It's been designed with Julia and her friends in mind—and for all of you who want to make sense of investing, even if you've tried before only to give up, feeling confused, overwhelmed, defeated, or bored. Or if you once believed you understood what to do only to be proven wrong.

As a remedy, we offer a few simple principles to help guide you to investment success. Throughout, we put you, the individual, at the center of the pursuit: you, your resources, your plans and, above all, your financial goals. These are the elements that should be driving your investment plan; and on these subjects *you* are the world's best expert.

At first blush, this may not sound terribly new or different. It's common practice, after all, for financial advisors to ask you all about your financial goals when they're preparing an investment plan for you.

But the goal-based investment paradigm is a game changer. It redefines the mission of personal finance. Your goals and your biography are not simply the stepping-off point for a plan. They are both driver and destination. They help determine the vehicle as well as the path. They dictate how high or low you can fly, how black-and-white your plan should be, and how much color or wiggle room you can add.

In contrast, conventional financial practices often take note of your goals but then seem to sideline them. In the conventional school, the route to goal achievement is indirect and often circuitous. Instead of goals, the objective is maximizing wealth. And the focus tends to be on the separate moving parts—as in selecting stocks and bonds, then aiming to beat each market benchmark.

This menu of choices can feel a little like building your own home computer system out of an array of separate components that may not serve your particular needs once they are assembled. Too often, making sure that your investments will meet your future needs has become your charge alone. In both cases, you are the one who will have to grapple with the pieces in order to impose the functionality you require. It's small wonder that frustrations can mount.

For most non-aficionados, separate computer components are too hard to orchestrate. It's easier to opt for the integrated desktop, or iPad, for that matter. Anything but plug-and-play feels difficult, because all we really care about is the applications—whether it's movies or spreadsheets.

The story is much the same when it comes to choosing goal-based investing over outdoing any given benchmark's return: What we ultimately care about is meeting our goals. You can't eat rate of return.

Paul subscribes to a goal-based investment philosophy. He believes that investing—and all financial planning— must be tailored to each individual's goals, resources, and opportunities. He's been influenced by life-cycle economics, and he considers lifestyle preservation at all stages of life to be of topmost importance.

At the group's next meeting, Paul introduces them to the core principles of goal-based investing. Right away, his framework brings their discussions down to earth. At once, they begin by looking at their own singularities, not their seemingly limitless investment possibilities.

Patrick is encouraged by the topic of conversation to move beyond his recent losses and to start talking about his personal financial goals. Soon, his friends press him to get more specific. When will he and Marianne be retiring? Where do they plan to live? How much might that cost? And so on.

Julia can see that she's now expected to stop grousing about her brothers and to put her questions about her recent inheritance on hold while she takes a closer look at her own bigger picture. She has to talk out loud now about how—and when—she plans to spend her money. When her turn to speak comes, she too feels pressed by the others to get realistic about attaching a price tag to her dreams, together with a timetable.

As Julia and Patrick ponder these questions, Sam points out how hard it is to put a price tag on goals like retirement that require resources over a long period. Up until his recent layoff, he admits, retirement seemed so far off to him that it was hard to make it a serious goal. If it hadn't been for the tax deferrals offered by his employer's retirement plan, he might never have started to set money aside. But unemployment changed that: As his job search stretched longer, he began to doubt whether he'd ever find work again.

Now that he's working again, Sam is still asking questions—but now he's wondering whether he'll ever be able to afford to retire. He has been reflecting quite a bit about how to protect his investments. He has a hard time, though, guessing how much money he'll need for retirement.

Sue agrees, and adds that even the cost of college has been hard to estimate as one future number. The idea that there is some elusive, magical number, she says, seems a little crazy. "All I want," she tells them, "is to be able to live the way I live now after I retire." There is a lot of agreement on this, but not a lot of discussion.

Paul jumps into the breach. He points out that there is room for more clarity and detail here, and proposes that they return to the subject in greater depth next time.

For now, he suggests, an overview is in order.

He points out that goals need to be feasible. He asks the group what makes the difference between a feasible goal and an unrealistic one.

The talk turns immediately to money. Not just money, but earnings and income. It's Julia's inheritance that has pointed the discussion in this direction; but, inevitably, the conversation soon turns to their pay. They're asked to consider how much they are earning, and also what they expect to earn over their lifetimes. Where are they in their careers? How predictable is their income? How flexible do they think they can be if faced with economic challenges?

Sue starts. As a physician, she expects a high degree of income security, but she feels that her savings so far are too small in comparison with her lifestyle and her goals. Still, she realizes that it has taken her until recently to pay off her debt from medical school and to save enough for her son's college tuition, so she expects to be able to have more money to invest in the future. She has yet to get a good grasp on what it will be like to be a divorced single mother.

Sam has a different take. He questions whether his old income expectations are ever going to pan out, even once the economy improves. He is toying with the idea of a career change. He reminds people of how decimated all his accounts still are, and concludes pessimistically that he plans to work for a long, long time.

Julia knows that her ability to save and invest is going to vary considerably from year to year. As the owner of a very small landscaping consultancy, she is hoping to grow but knows she can't count on it. That's the reason she has wanted to avoid risk when investing her inheritance. She's been troubled by feedback she's had that she needs to take risk if she wants to net enough money to pay for education and retirement.

Julia's husband, a tenured high school teacher, has a stable and predictable income. But it has amounted to less than half their joint income and Julia, ever uneasy, worries they may be living beyond their means.

Patrick feels as though time is not on his side because he has fewer years left in the workforce than the others in the group. He acknowledges how much pain the collapse of 2008 caused him and Marianne. He wants to map out different ways he might be able to reach his goals over a 10-year time horizon. Although his income is stable and relatively secure, the brevity of his time frame worries him.

In these conversations, Julia and her friends have reframed their investment projects in simple, clear, and personally meaningful terms. Taking a goal-based view has led them to consider both their desired outcomes and their expected inputs. Their thinking about investment has turned immediate and concrete.

Reframing Risk

So far, we've introduced you to the starting point of goal-based investing, showing how a twin focus on an individual's desired outcomes and expected income leads to a clear, concrete agenda. But this is just the beginning. When you take stock of your goals in terms of the annual cash distributions they will require, as Sam and Sue have proposed, you're also well on your way toward solving the hardest part of the investment puzzle—deciding how much risk is right for you.

That's because goal-based investing encourages matching your investments today to your future needs. And the matching structure reframes risk in a new way.

Now that you are focusing on required yearly spending instead of a more abstract notion of target asset value, it's a quick intuitive jump to envision just how much a given shortfall will hurt. Changing the yardstick for measuring risk in this way also shines a spotlight on it. Loss has a context. Your grasp of potential shortfalls is tighter than it seemed before.

For instance, if you experience serious portfolio losses, that nice check you've been planning to cash from your retirement fund—the one that's meant to cover living expenses over and above Social Security each year in retirement—could be reduced to a much smaller amount.

For perspective, in this past decade of two collapsed stock market bubbles, stock market losses in the trusty S&P

index, when adjusted for inflation, averaged just over a nickel on every dollar each and every year. If you had accumulated a nice balance in an S&P index fund at the start of the decade, more than half of it, in buying-power terms, would have vanished.

Of course, if you had needed to spend that money, your living-expense budget would have had to shrink by the same measure. You get the picture. The process of weighing investments against specific goals can concentrate the mind wonderfully.

The conventional answer to managing potential losses is to bet the odds, diversify, stay invested for the long term, and hope for the best.

But you're a person, not an institution; you plan on spending what you need when you need it. And there's the rub. Even if you have some flexibility to postpone your goals, your time horizon is not terribly elastic. Your child needs

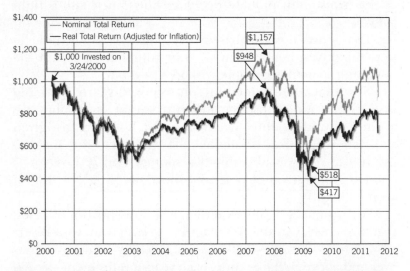

Figure 1.1   S&P Total Return and Real Total Return on $1,000 Invested on March 24, 2000
Returns Include Reinvested Dividends
Source: Doug Short, Advisor Perspectives. Used with permission.

to attend college within a narrow window of time; you may postpone retirement, to be sure, but not indefinitely.

Instead of taking the conventional approach, try flipping the risk question on its head and think about what you *cannot* afford to lose. This may equate to the amounts you have targeted for your goals; but most likely you can reimagine your destinations in their most essential terms, separating wants from basic needs.

How low can you turn down the jets? Is a state or community college a viable alternative to a private university? Can you find frills and extras you may be able to do without during retirement if you must? Perhaps your bare essential living expense budget can go lower. It may help to subject your goals to a series of virtual crash tests to find your own bright line between "must-haves" and "nice-to-haves."

This sharp edge is your line of defense. It's the part of your investment portfolio that belongs in safer instruments. We'll talk at greater length about what constitutes a safer investment, and we'll show you how best to acquire them. For now, the critical point is that you can build a self-made hedging plan that's sure to cover your most basic goals.

A hedge is a tradeoff. To protect your basic needs, you can cut your exposure to loss by investing in safer instruments. When you hedge in this way, you don't pay anything, but you give up possible extra gains beyond the yield of your safe investments.

How much you allocate to safe instruments will be one of your most important decisions. It's important not to decide in a vacuum, but to tie your safe investments to the essential needs you must protect.

Before we leave the subject of risk reframing, let's return for a moment to our starting point, as Julia and her group are taking turns specifying both their goals and their funding sources. You'll recall that everyone recognized how closely their earnings power defined the amounts they could invest. No surprise there, because income from work is where most people get the bulk of their resources.

But here's an added point that's easy to overlook: Your earning power—its stability and flexibility in particular—also sheds light on your ability to take risk. Again, this is intuitive, yet it's an observation that's commonly ignored. That is a real shame, because it is so easy to build your earnings expectations into your personal risk prescription.

Try comparing yourself to the friends in the support group, for example. Sam realizes that the unpredictability of working in a smaller company probably means that he already has added risk to his plate. Spooked by a long period of unemployment, he has already incorporated his intuition into his personal risk profile.

Patrick had once felt secure as a seasoned human-resources manager with a great deal of seniority in the drug company that employs him. But he no longer does. He's concerned that he and his wife Marianne no longer have enough working years ahead of them to replenish their diminished savings. But his anxiety may be leading him in the wrong direction. While his risk-taking habits in the past might have made sense in light of his secure income and his younger age, circumstances have changed. Paul is trying to show Patrick that he is playing with fire.

Sue, on the other hand, recognizes that as a pediatrician her income is relatively stable, substantial, and predictable. From that perspective, she may once have had a fair amount of unused risk capacity. On the other hand, she is about to be newly divorced. Her ex-husband will be making cash contributions toward her children's education needs, but he'll only partially cover them. And for her retirement, Sue is now relying exclusively on her own earning power, so she does not have extra risk capacity after all.

That may be the case for Julia, too, despite her inheritance. As a small-business owner, Julia's earning expectations are neither stable nor predictable. Still, as a successful entrepreneur with professional skills, she has a career path that is flexible and probably resilient. And her husband's income, while lower than hers, is relatively secure. So Julia's case is not cut-and-dried.

The younger members of the group are in their thirties or forties and can look forward to a long working life ahead of them. As time passes, though, the future income they can expect over their lifetime horizons will naturally start to shrink, and this will reduce their ability to take investment risks. This is what Patrick and Marianne need to understand, too.

Our starting focus on outcomes and incomes has turned into a powerful springboard to reconsider risk on a very personal basis. It can facilitate matching on two fronts, between future goals and planned investments and also between earnings power and recommended risk. We'll have much more to say about ways to recalibrate risk as we proceed.

Let's join Julia and her group as they learn how to put their investments on a firmer footing. They'll be building on the central premise that personal finance is about you—your goals, your values, your family, and your career path. The rest is secondary. And that's where we'll turn next: your self-assessment, starting with your goals in all their distinctive detail.

CHAPTER 2

Picturing Your Destination

*If you don't know where you are going, you'll end up
someplace else.*

—Yogi Berra

It seems a small order, asking you to list your personal
financial goals. And, in fact, it is quite easy for most people
who are asked by their financial advisors to complete the
traditional questionnaire.

Yet, developing a clear picture of your financial destinations can be anything but simple, especially when you try to
push beyond vague generalizations to get into the specifics.

The Challenge

It's the rare young person who wants to envisage a gray-haired
dotage in a distant future; and it's the rare individual who
actually sets down cherished financial aspirations in writing.

Most of the barriers to goal setting can be chalked up
to a failure of imagination. No question about it: Events
that will take place in the future can be elusive—the farther

away, the more unreal. It's truly difficult to drum up interest in events that seem remote or unpredictable.

Take education. No matter how committed you are as a parent, it's still taxing to foresee higher-education options for the young child whose future ambitions can't yet be read. And—consistent with the common delusion that "everyone ages but me"—it can be hard to see past an ocean of time to admit that we will one day reach retirement age.

Shorter-term goals, too, have a habit of eclipsing longer-term propositions. If you suspect unspoken family disagreements around goals, you may shrink from articulating them to avoid strife. And we can even harbor dueling goals without realizing they're in conflict.

Since your goals will be driving your investment decisions, you want to get this part right. The more clearly you can picture your goals, the better equipped you will be to meet them.

You don't have to get it perfect on the first try. The uncertainty of a long planning horizon doesn't have to hold you back—it's not a test, but an opportunity to set the right *direction* and get you on your way. Start now. The momentum you create can help you recognize and resolve any conflicts that may be immobilizing you. There will be plenty of time to correct your course.

Try the "target practice" exercises in this chapter and use them as tools to revisit in the future. A one-time bull's-eye would be foolish, even arrogant, to attempt—as well as near impossible. It's a journey, not a single shot. The closer we get to the destination, the closer we need to be to the course—but at the outset, it's the direction that counts.[1]

Target Practice in Six Easy Steps

The secret to setting reachable goals is hidden in the details: the more specific the goal, the easier to pursue. And the most winning approach incorporates discipline and imagination in equal measure. Aim to visualize your destinations in bright colors and high resolution. After all, these are aspirations that you care about. But you also want to stick with goals that are achievable, so that you can turn them from wishes and desires into goals and plans. This is not the time for magical thinking.

In the exercise that follows, we'll walk you through a "target practice" to help you out. Here are six easy steps toward setting your financial goals:

Imagine your destination.
Monitor your progress.
Prioritize your needs.
Assign a time line.
Consult with key partners.
Tally the costs.

The exercise is organized for impact. To get started, lead with your imagination.

Step 1: Imagine Your Destination

You need nothing but a pen, some paper, and an active mind. Write down all the material goals that are important to you. Beneath each goal you jot down, leave space for descriptive comments that highlight the centerpiece elements you're seeking.

For example, if your goal is to purchase a new home, add the features you most want. In your descriptive sections, include a line or two about your principal purpose in choosing the goal. What's the purpose behind that house you hope to buy? Are you looking for a better school district, or is it a need for more space that's driving you?

What about retirement? What purposes do you have in mind? Most likely, you want to maintain your customary lifestyle even after you stop receiving a paycheck from your employer. Do you want to start an encore career? Do you plan to travel? In other words, give some thought to whether you plan to consume more or less than you do today.

Most Common Financial Goals

Create an emergency fund
Retire at age 68
Start/build education fund for child(ren)
Buy, build, or remodel a home
Maintain long-term care insurance
Maintain disability insurance
Plan a major vacation
Buy expensive items (car, boat, RV)
Buy a vacation home
Change careers

At this stage in your goal setting, it is helpful to add clarity while subtracting unnecessary distractions. Focusing on your purpose along with your key requirements will help you do both.

You won't be too surprised to see that the most popular financial goals are limited to fewer than a dozen broad categories. But this does not make cookie-cutters out of them. It's how you color each goal that will make your list uniquely your own.

You'll note that we haven't included some frequently mentioned items like "set up a 401(k) at work," or "save $100 every week," which are better characterized as paths toward other, longer-term financial goals. If you are having trouble making this distinction, then the next steps in this target practice may help you separate your planned routes from your list of destinations. Remember, your list doesn't have to be long.

There is one goal, however, that must appear on every list, whether you are 64 or 24 years old. And that's the goal of retiring. Even if you plan to join the Supreme Court and work until age 90, there will come a time, no matter how much you love your work, when you'll no longer be able to count fully on your income from employment.

Of course, the farther from retirement you are, the harder it is to paint yourself a clear picture. The imponderables are too many. Time, place, marital status, and lifestyle—these may all feel like enormous unknowns. If this small sketch describes you, don't just shrug your shoulders and walk away. At a minimum, create a retirement placeholder. Adjustments can come later.

Early money packs a big wallop. The earlier you start, the earlier you can retire. But you have to *act* early.

If you started late or haven't started yet, don't be chagrined. Being late is better than being broke. But don't wait. There is no time like the present. Shakespeare's Richard II learned this too late and could only lament, "I wasted time, and now doth time waste me."

Step 2: Monitor Your Progress

As you proceed with your targeting, remember that your list is sure to evolve. Some goals will drop off your horizon as you achieve them, others may change radically over time, and still others will sharpen in focus as they approach. This understanding takes the pressure off, because it allows you to work with rough approximations and to continue making adjustments as needed.

It also underlines the value of a periodic review of your list of goals—perhaps as often as once a year. You'll be reviewing your list to be sure it's current, to make modifications if necessary, and to fill in your broad brushstrokes with more detail and more intense colors when you can.

Step 3: Prioritize Your Needs

Not all goals are created equal. It's important to distinguish high-priority goals from others. Once you've prepared your list, take a moment to rank each item in order of importance. Don't let indecision slow you down.

Unfortunately, it's easy to confuse distant goals with low-priority ones. As a result, many people ascribe a low

Table 2.1   Sample Form for Setting Goal Priorities

Goal	Description	Rank
Goal #1	Retire at age 67	1
Goal #2	Build college fund for oldest child	2
Goal #3	Build college fund for younger child	2
Goal #4	Down payment for house purchase	4

importance to retirement when it seems far away. But some far-off goals need close attention even if they are hard to imagine right now. Just because retirement may be a long way off doesn't mean it can rank low on your list.

Here is a simple example of how priority rankings can help you focus on what's most important.

One device that can help you avoid procrastinating when your deadlines seem distant is to ask yourself whether a goal represents a need—something you must have in order to live—or whether it's something you want. Needs are the bare essentials: a roof over your head, clothing, food, water, and what it takes to maintain good health.

Of course, the line between needs and wants, the nonnegotiable essentials and discretionary items, can blur. Different people will answer the wants-or-needs question differently. Take good health and nutrition. One person will eat healthy food on a moderate budget while another may believe that expensive organic fruits and vegetables are essential.

Some things are essential for everyone. Everyone needs enough income to live on in old age. And it's not just old age—each and every one of us may be forced to retire unexpectedly, whether because of the economy, poor health, or family circumstances beyond our control. So retirement is a need, not a want, and this makes it automatically trump all goals in the list that line up in the "nice to have" column but don't appear as "must-haves."

If you are tempted to ignore retirement as a high-priority goal, remember too that catching up later will be hard to do.

The setback will be even greater if you choose not to exploit any tax-deferred retirement accounts you may have at work, because these allow your money to accumulate tax free until withdrawal.

The wants-or-needs distinction is also a good way to set priorities within each of your goals. For each goal, try to distinguish your bare minimum needs from the things you want but don't strictly need. For an example, look at Julia's attempt to distinguish her basic requirements during retirement from what she really would like her golden years to look like.

It helps to reality-test your results by picturing your future in as much detail as possible. Have you inadvertently skimped so that the minimal baseline you've described isn't really feasible? Have you left out anything essential for health care or long-term care insurance needs? Or have you gone overboard in the opposite direction by including features you really can live without? This is a less likely concern, but one to think about.

This distinction between needs and wants will point you toward your rock-bottom baseline—the level of future income your investments *must* safely yield. It is the bright

Table 2.2   Wants and Needs in Retirement: Julia's List

Essential Needs in Retirement	Wants in Retirement
Basic shelter	Comfortable, spacious housing; home cleaning service
Basic utilities (heating, water, electricity, phone, and cell phone service)	Utilities (heating, air conditioning; Internet and cable; telephone and cell phone service)
Basic groceries	High-quality food; dining out weekly
Basic clothing	Fashionable, well-made clothing;
Health insurance coverage	Health club/tennis club membership
Basic transportation	New car every 5–7 years; travel each year
Entertainment: Use the public library	Theatre, concerts, movies

red line of defense we described in Chapter 1, and it will be a central consideration when you decide how to invest.[2]

Step 4: Assign a Time Line

Step 4 should be a very quick stride to take. Tie your goals to deadlines. If you can't name a specific date, or if it makes no sense to do so, choose a range instead. Without tying down a time line, you have nothing but a wish list blowing in the wind. From a psychological standpoint, too, deadlines add the crucial element of motivation.

Compare Julia and Sue's education investment plans. Julia acknowledges that she plans to invest for her children's education. "For me, educating my children is a big reason for investing today," she says. She leaves it at that, open-ended, although she surely knows her children's ages and expected times of graduation from high school.

Sue, on the other hand, shares Julia's goals but she's already focusing on specific dates, as depicted in Figure 2.1.

Listen to the way a deadline concentrates the mind and brings a goal closer to fruition. "Now that my oldest son has started college, I have become newly aware that I have just 10 years before my 8-year-old is ready for college," Sue says. "And my 11-year-old will graduate from high school three years before her. If they both go to college, as I expect, then we'll have one year when we need to help out with two different tuition bills. On top of that, we have tuition bills right now—and for the next 4 years—for my oldest. So we are keeping our eyes on the next 4 years, as well as on the period that's 7 to 14 years away."

Julia and Sue have children who are in elementary school. As long as Julia's thinking floats timelessly off-calendar, it will

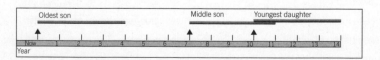

Figure 2.1   Time Line for Sue's College Goals

remain vague. By contrast, Sue has been forced to attention by having an older child in college. She has set two separate time frames. Even though the second is seven years away and surrounded with uncertainty, it has become much more vivid in her mind. As a result, Sue is poised for action but Julia is not.

Step 5: Consult with Key Partners

Your goals are the mainspring of your investment plan. So, unless you lead a solitary existence, it's worth consulting with the key partners in your life to reach consensus about the financial goals you share.

Often, goals don't get formulated well because they conceal unexpressed conflicts. One spouse may want to retire early, but the other may have entirely different intentions. One may wish to travel during retirement, the other simply to be near family. One may wish to fund a child's entire education costs, but the other may insist on having the child assume more responsibility.

Difficult subjects don't end there. Discussions about relocating to a new city or caring for elderly parents can be especially prickly. Other family members' opinions may bear considerable weight depending on the situation.

This is not the stuff of finance, but it's a matter that you can't afford to overlook. If you take this target practice together with important partners in your life, you may get halfway to consensus and beyond.

Step 6: Tally Costs

The last step is a critical one—attaching a price tag to your goals. Money talks. Completing this exercise can finally catapult your dreams into planning terrain.

This can be a challenging research project, but you don't have to let it spin out of control. There are plenty of efficient shortcuts. Check out the abbreviated cheat sheet we've added to help you complete your initial research quickly. Later, you can return and add detail as you require.

Table 2.3   Resources for Estimating the Costs of Common Goals

Goal	Information Resources
Buying a home	Home valuation web sites; local banks (mortgage rates and requirements); municipal web sites (for property tax rolls, which usually include assessments and tax rate information)
Higher education	Web sites of individual colleges and universities; family conversations about what level of funding you plan to provide; IRS Publication 970 ("Tax Benefits for Education")
Retirement	Use your current consumption as a benchmark; your most recent income tax return; web site of the Social Security Administration; web site of the AARP

One thing you won't be able to predict is future inflation (or deflation), so let's be clear: The numbers you are assigning are in today's dollars. In subsequent chapters, we'll talk more about how to align today's dollars (or "real" dollars) with the actual (or nominal) costs.

As you conduct your resource analysis, extract the cost of your basic needs as well as your wants. The line between them, in today's dollars, brings us back to your bright line of defense from risk. It's the minimum you must be assured of having when the time comes to spend—and, again, it signals how much you need to have in safe investments.

Now that you've reached the end of this targeting exercise, you're ready to consolidate your results. On one sheet of paper, list your goals, the resources they will require, their priority, and estimated timing. The six-step exercise toward IMPACT can help keep longer-term goals in focus alongside more imminent ones. It also allows you to visualize—and eliminate—potential conflicts among your goals. For instance, too many short-term goals with too high a price tag may not be feasible. Seeing them side by side in your list might set you rethinking your priorities and timing to better effect.

Hold on to your outline. It's not just a baseline for you to return to in future years. It's a travel guide to keep your destinations in clear and constant view.

Defining Success

Establishing financial goals is a necessary starting point for all personal investors. But in the goal-based investing approach that we're advocating, your goals not only set the table—they determine the menu. And they also provide the best rating criterion imaginable.

With all the noise in the marketplace about performance, it's easy to get distracted from this fundamental fact. The standard of success is not a comparison with a market index or composite. These work well for evaluating professional money managers. But they fluctuate constantly and serve only to weigh your results against various market averages. When it comes to judging your own personal investment performance, it's your goals that make the most meaningful benchmarks. The proof of the pudding is in the eating. And the definition of success lies in the achieving.

Sam and Sue Lay Out Their Goals

To help model your targets, let's see how Sam and Sue have completed their IMPACT target practice. We'll walk through the form that each produced.

Sue is focused right now on ensuring that she can provide an education for her three children. Since her eldest is already a student at the state university, she's already had the experience, with her ex-husband, of signing some big checks, and she has already developed a good idea of the resources they will need.

When she first tried her target practice, you won't be surprised that she chose "education" as her first-priority goal. She broke her education objectives into three separate goals, one for each child. And she assigned an equal priority to each, even though she expected two of the tuition payment streams to come due later than the first, as you can see from her time line in Figure 2.1.

By instinct, she initially assigned a rank of "4" to retirement, placing it after the education of her three children. She saw it as

(Continued)

paling in significance when compared to the looming costs of sending three students to college. But on reflection, and after some prodding from Paul, she realized that her retirement—if only at an initial bare minimum level—was her number one priority since it was an essential need, not discretionary at all. So she revised her rankings. Retirement would come first, education second.

Although Sue insisted, quite properly, on assigning the same priority to each child, her egalitarianism doesn't require her to set money aside in equal amounts for each of them if this is hard. Since she has 10 more years until her youngest graduates from high school, she has more years to catch up. But she has put retirement funding first—*at least at a minimal level of resources*. She will be taking advantage of tax-deferred retirement plans and possibly tax-advantaged Roth plans.

Sam zeroed in on retirement as his foremost investment goal. He is behaving unusually for someone in his late thirties, but as he told his friends, being unemployed for 9 months really spooked him. At first, Sam thought that buying a house was a good idea with prices down, and that his second goal would be to accumulate enough money for a down payment in the next 3 to 5 years. His third goal was also a short-term one—to accumulate enough money for a new car, which he considered a need and not a want, because his office was not accessible by public transportation.

On further deliberation, Sam realized that the car was more important to him than the house. Reflecting on the priorities question made him realize that he needs the car but not the house. He decided he was willing to buy a less expensive or used car if he could find a fuel-efficient one in reasonable shape. He could pay for it outright or with a down payment and a 3-year loan. Any extra money he saves he can invest toward the house down payment. But he has not ruled out a new, more comfortable car.

Sam completed his list by adding a category he wants to flag, although it still seems like a big unknown—marrying and having a family. For now, he has decided to invest only very small amounts toward that goal—but he wants a cushion in case his circumstances change soon. (He hopes they will.)

Picturing Your Destination   29

When Paul reviewed their conclusions, he suggested that each of them had forgotten to think about emergencies. He also encouraged Sue to increase the size of her life insurance policy as part of her regular living expenses, now that she is a single parent. And he urged them both to build up an emergency fund to cover half a year's spending before they invested toward their other goals.

Sue's Goals

Needs	Cost Today	Wants	Cost Today	Rank	Target Dates
Education for oldest child at state college—supplemented by his financial aid and part-time work	$12,000 per year	Education for oldest child at state college debt free	$20,000–$24,000 per year	3	Next 4 years
Retirement at basic levels	2/3 of current income per year	Comfortable retirement	80% of current income per year	2	Age 70 (in 21 years)
Education for middle child at state college—supplemented by his financial aid and part-time work	$12,000 per year	Education for middle child at state college debt free	$20,000–$24,000 per year or more	3	In 7 years for a period of 4 years
Education for youngest child at state college—supplemented by her financial aid and part-time work	$12,000 per year	Education for youngest child at state college debt free	$20,000–$24,000 per year or more	3	In 10 years for a period of 4 years
Fund an emergency precautionary savings stash	Expenses for half a year	n/a	n/a	1	Immediately

(Continued)

Sam's Goals

Needs	Cost Today	Wants	Cost Today	Rank	Target Dates
Fund an emergency precautionary savings stash	Expenses for half a year	n/a	n/a	1	Immediately
Basic retirement	70% of current income	Comfortable retirement	A guess only; more than 70% of current income; Sam will revisit in the future	2	At least 25 years from now (with luck)
Car	$18,000–$24,000	Latest hybrid car comfortable enough for long trips and commutes	$24,000–$38,000	3	12 to 24 months
War chest for future change in lifestyle	Unknown; aims to defer 5% of spending	War chest for future change in lifestyle	Unknown; aims to defer more than 5% of spending	4	5 to 7 years away

CHAPTER

Paying Up

Good thoughts are no better than good dreams, unless they be executed.

—Ralph Waldo Emerson

Congratulations. You have managed to create a vivid picture of your financial destinations, no small accomplishment. But the work is only partly done. You also need to make sure that you can pay your way. You can transform your passions into reality only if you have the means to pay for them. Without reliable resources to foot the bill, you've just been window-shopping—your wish lists by themselves can't buy a thing.

Where do we look for all the wealth that's needed to make your goals real?

From Dreaming to Planning

Depending on how much get-rich-quick snake oil you have brushed up against, you may be surprised to learn that your foremost source of money—the one that will ultimately pay

31

for the bulk of your material needs—is your job. More precisely, it is your ability to earn a living—and your prospective lifetime earnings from work. For most households, earnings dwarf income from all other sources.

There is a widely used economic term for this power. The value of an individual's prospective lifetime earnings from work is called "human capital." Perhaps you've encountered this phrase before.

The three operative words here are "lifetime," "prospective," and "work." Together, they signal that your future income from *work* is a crucial factor in determining your lifetime wealth. It's not for naught that Warren Buffett continues to stress that "the best investment you can make is in yourself."

In addition, it is sensible to make consumption and savings decisions based on your expectations of your *lifetime* earnings, and not just on the basis of your current income. When imagining your lifetime earnings, start with your income expectations and their growth as well as their variability.

But think, too, about other traits of your earnings profile. How resilient or inflexible is your income in case of economic disruptions? How predictable? If you are a tenured college professor or an established physician, your expected income is reasonably predictable and secure. But if you're a real estate broker, a social worker, or an unemployed older worker, you're much more vulnerable. And your income security has a direct bearing on how much lifetime income you can conservatively anticipate.

Finally, planning is by necessity *dynamic*. This is a caveat we've seen before, and it applies to saving as well as to spending. Gauging your *prospective* lifetime earnings from work involves a fair amount of guesswork. People in certain professions can anticipate more predictability than others, but each and every one of us has to expect the unexpected. Future income is not certain for anyone. So, as your circumstances change, you'll need to keep revising your plan. And you'll also want to keep reserving funds for unforeseen surprises.

Your Ability to Earn a Living and Your Investment Goals

Your lifetime earnings from work are the major source of your personal wealth and the principal determinant of your lifestyle.

Your decisions about how much to spend now—and how much later—make the most sense when you weigh them broadly, over the sweep of a lifetime, and in light of your lifelong earnings expectations.

Your profile as breadwinner can take many shapes. Your earning ability can be predictable or uncertain, resilient or inflexible. You can balance many of its features by choosing investments that have offsetting characteristics.

View your goals and decisions dynamically, especially because your ability to earn a living can suffer unexpected ups and downs.

This depiction of your earning power as the principal engine for realizing your financial goals may seem intuitive and obvious. Yet it's surprisingly absent from a great deal of investment advice. Instead, plenty of traditional advice leaps from an initial snapshot of your goals right to suggestions about how to earn the return that's required to meet them.

It's a hazardous omission.

To get a better feel for how misleading your results would be if you paid scant attention to your earning power over the sweep of a whole lifetime, consider a successful young athlete who can expect very high earnings over a horizon of, say, 15 years. Or picture a child actor, or a lottery winner.

Beyond their ample current incomes, what these three share is an extremely uncertain future. Yet, each expects to keep up a lifestyle to match their high income. You would not advise them to adopt the same financial plan as a top physician with a comparable income but with close to 40 years to practice, would you? You'd almost certainly encourage them to think about spreading their wealth well into the future.

Viewing your life—and your lifetime earnings—in alignment with your material ambitions is one of the best ways to arrive at an investment portfolio that fits *you*. By integrating

> *Human capital:* This is what economists call the value today (or the
> present value) of an individual's future labor income. Human
> capital can be viewed from the perspective of an employer, but
> here we are interested in it from the point of view of the individual
> earner and investor. Although human capital is intangible, and
> can't be directly bought or sold, it's a major source of each indi-
> vidual's lifetime wealth.

your sources and uses of money, you shine a light on plans
that are beyond your means. Overreaching is easier to spot, so
setting right-sized investment goals becomes more clear-cut.

And by projecting this unified, income-based outlook
across the full length of your life, you put the trade-offs
between current and future spending in perspective.

Finally, because this alignment allows you to envision
your overall wealth holistically, as a blend of your financial
and human resources, it also provides an important anchor
for managing risk. In general, the greater your uncertainty
about future income, the more you should restrict risky
investments.

Let's look more closely at how these ideas can work in
practice.[1]

Different Kinds of Capital

Let's start by visualizing the relationship between your lifetime earnings and your goals. On paper, try mapping out
the path you expect your own lifetime income to follow—up
until the day you leave the workforce. Don't be overly concerned with precision. It's a long horizon, maybe extremely
long—and you're only estimating, based on the best knowledge you have today.

Some comfort for those allergic to numbers: These estimation guides are pretty basic, but if they are not for you,
skip the drill. Do read through the exercise though. You'll

still be able to visualize the concepts, and you can work your own numbers later with the help of an advisor if you choose.

Make your estimates in today's dollars. That way, you avoid the conundrum of guessing future inflation. Instead, by using today's dollars, the idea is to show "real" dollars, with unchanging purchasing power, just as you did in the last chapter. This means that any income growth you anticipate should leave out adjustments for inflation. Stick with today's purchasing power.

Your number series can be expressed as a single total "present" value today.* It represents your human capital.

Here's the key takeaway. If you want a good handle on your total wealth, you must include your income potential. Your human capital combined with your financial assets (or your financial capital) add up to your total wealth.

Unless you are quite near retirement, your human capital figure probably comes to a rather large amount, and an unfamiliar one at that. We're not accustomed to thinking about our future earnings potential as one big bundle of value. It's also true that human capital is intangible—it can't be directly bought or sold, touched or traded. It represents potential, not current, income. You can't deposit it directly in the bank. The run-of-the-mill bean counter may miss it entirely.

Still, because your earning power is such an important source of your overall wealth and well-being, we need to pay a lot of attention to it. It gives you a handy, single reference point—much like the posted price of a bond that you can buy today in exchange for an income flow over future years.

---

*The value today is usually lower than the sum of all the numbers because money has a "time value." A dollar today is worth a dollar plus *interest* in a year. If the interest rate is greater than zero, a dollar today is therefore worth more next year, and still more in 2 years' time. This is the simple relationship behind the notion of "present value." However, if you assume that the real rate of interest is close to zero, as it is right now, then you don't need to make any calculations at all to arrive at an inflation-adjusted present value.

Now for a parallel set of estimates—this time on the spending side of your life. On a second page, map the course you expect your lifetime expenditures to take. As a guideline, you might return to the preliminary lifetime budget you sketched out when you estimated your retirement budget goals in Chapter 2.

For the numbers-resistant, skip the exercise but read on to catch the concepts. This can be an excellent task to perform with a financial planner, if you're working with one. Remember to stick with today's dollars and today's purchasing power for now. Remember, too, to layer in your goals and the spending they will require, whether these occur during retirement or before. Your time frame in this instance will be a lifetime horizon that extends well beyond the time line on your labor income map.

In fact, the divergent time horizons of income and spending describe the core investment challenge in a nutshell: The object of the game is not to accumulate riches for their own sake, but to spread wealth from years when there is a surplus to years when the money coming in may not be enough.

You can easily translate this cash flow series into its corresponding "present" value today. This exercise allows you to visualize the connection between your human capital and your financial goals. As you review your own profile, remind yourself not to sweat the details. Don't squander time capturing the fine points. At the outset, approximations are more than sufficient.

Even if you prefer to postpone this exercise, take a look at the sample lifetime balance sheet in Figure 3.1. It clearly depicts a young family—or individual—well positioned to match their lifetime wherewithal with their life expenditures. Both the assets and the liabilities represent the present values of expected cash flows in the future.

You may be surprised at first to see your planned spending lined up on the Liability side of the ledger. After all, as Patrick insisted, this list represented his goals and dreams; he considered them a plus and not a liability. But recall that

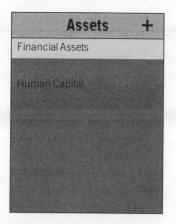 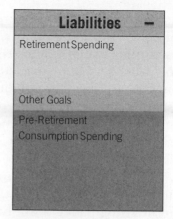

Figure 3.1   A Lifetime Balance Sheet

your goals must be paid for or they'll remain only dreams. Consider them payments that you owe to yourself.

In this example, assets and liabilities are neatly matched. It's possible to imagine a wobbly balance sheet, though, where liabilities exceed assets. That misfortune would require you to restore equilibrium. You might try revising spending— including future goals—downward. Or, a more palatable solution could be to find a reliable way to boost your assets— say, by working longer and retiring later.

On the other hand, assets can also exceed liabilities, leaving a surplus and a legacy for future heirs. Or, depending on preferences, a surplus can permit you to upgrade your spending instead.

In other words, your personal lifetime balance sheet provides a clear, visual gauge of how feasible your goals are. It helps you think through potential revisions and trade-offs. And by showing your financial portfolio alongside your human wealth, it captures your whole, lifelong wealth in one picture.

If you are reading this template very closely, you may have noticed that, to keep things simple, we have left out potential payments from defined benefit pension plans and Social

Security. If you'd like to figure these in, using constant "present value" dollars, then you'll want to place them on the Assets side of your balance sheet. (Another way to approach this is simply to net expected Social Security payments from your future spending liabilities during retirement.) These resources can be categorized as "non-human" capital. The same would be true of any money you may expect to inherit, which we've also omitted for simplicity's sake, and which also falls into the same category.

Now imagine your balance sheet at a future date. It's going to look quite different, because your spending, saving, and investing patterns will have changed and all these have a dramatic effect on your wealth.

Each year a little of your human capital morphs from an intangible into actual money. As you draw on your human capital over time, your prospective earnings become actual earnings while human capital declines.

What you save and invest, though, remains part of your total wealth—it simply moves from the intangible "human capital" column into your financial portfolio. As long as you continue to save—and to invest safely—your *financial* capital should keep growing, even as you draw down your human capital.

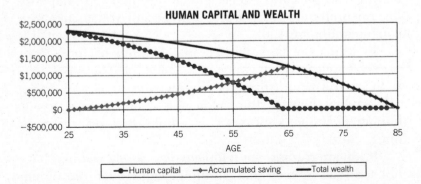

Figure 3.2   Lifetime Human Capital and Wealth

Visualizing the evolution of your personal balance sheet over a lifetime reinforces the message. The lifestyle you expect to maintain throughout needs to correspond with your lifelong resources.

Creating a Lifetime Budget

We can translate this information from the personal balance sheet into a lifetime budget and investment strategy. Each of your goals requires cash—making each a liability—which we know must be funded, ultimately, from your human capital. What goal-based investing does is to match the money you save with the money you will need to meet your goals. It's as simple and straightforward as that: Match your cash investments today to the extra cash you require tomorrow.

And because you've already estimated how much money each goal will require, as well as the specific dates when the money will be spent, there is little mystery involved.

To see how this might work, let's shuttle from your balance sheet back to your projected cash flows. Let's return to your expected income, saving, and spending in future years. For a year-by-year take, you can observe how earning, saving, and spending play out as time goes by in Figure 3.3.

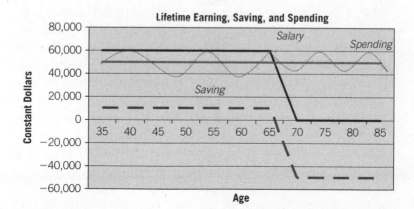

Figure 3.3   Lifetime Earning, Saving, and Spending

If you find you have the wherewithal to fund all your lifetime goals safely, earning a very small but safe inflation-adjusted interest rate, then your work is done. If, on the other hand, your current needs are making your later goals seem unattainable, it's time to revise your plan.

Chances are you'll wind up somewhere in between these two extremes. You probably won't be able to safely cover all your lifetime goals—but you will most likely be able to fund at least your basic needs.

To cover your minimal spending needs when they come due, create a safe investing zone. (We'll talk more about the details of your safety zone in Part III, along with the best instruments to choose at different stages of life.) Your aspirational goals—the desires that you're willing to give up if necessary—can be funded through risky investments.

Matching financial assets to future liabilities doesn't mean matching in stages—that is, ignoring later goals such as retirement until you've achieved earlier ones. The best plans will be guided first by the priorities you've attached to your goals. Only then does timing come into play. Remember Sue, who realized she could not defer retirement saving until after her kids' college—but who understood, too, that she didn't have to pay equally into three college funds at once.

We'll be filling in many more practical details about how to match your assets with your liabilities. At this point, we want to introduce you to this powerful concept, underline some of its principal advantages, and show how matching can solve some shortcomings of more conventional strategies.

One benefit lies in the clear vantage point you get on your progress and prospects. In the last chapter, we saw the advantages of using financial goals to define success. Goals are a meaningful way to measure personal progress. Now, with this next step—adding human capital to the assessment—you get an accessible view of your prospects. What is your guesstimate of the total resources you can rely on, and will there be enough to let you go the distance?

In comparison, rate-of-return reporting—which you may see on your monthly statements but which is unhinged from your personal profile—is not as informative.

Another advantage of matching is in the confidence you gain that you can cover your future minimum spending needs, because you'll be investing in right-sized and safe instruments.

This confidence is justified because it's rooted in a personalized, nuanced view of your future spending and saving. By visualizing how your earnings potential will get actualized, and then pairing that picture with a forecast of your future spending needs, you've also charted a nice sketch of your financial position in different stages of your life.

These stages become shorthand for the life patterns you plan to pursue. They'll be handy for guiding your spending and investment decisions, and your risk levels in particular, over time.

Considering this nuance, the message is not that you must "save at all costs." You're plainly aiming to transfer resources, as robustly and sensibly as you can, from fat years to leaner ones.

But, depending on your lifetime situation, there could be times when spending today unambiguously beats the alternatives. Given the benefits of clarity and confidence, you should be able to tell the difference.

Maybe you are lucky enough that your goals are already within striking distance, with ample resources still to come and no dependents or heirs on the horizon to think about. As prudent as it is to save, it could be foolish to cut your current spending unnecessarily. We are not channeling Ben Franklin on saving and thrift, virtuous as both may seem.

Insights from Behavioral Finance

Interestingly, studies have shown that managing your money in separate accounts—and according to your different life-time goals—accords well with the way people tend to think about investing. This psychological insight originates with behavioral economists, not with traditional finance theorists or life-cycle economists, and it has led some of them to promote goal-based investing as a result.

The approach we are advocating has an entirely different source of inspiration, as we've explained. Because the overlap is undeniable, though, let's zero in on the behavioral view of goal-based investing.

In bygone days, before personal computers and widespread retail banking, many households put their paycheck dollars each week directly into different jars for safekeeping. There was a jar for the rent, one for groceries, one for the electric bill, and so on. It made intuitive sense and seemed a prudent way to make ends meet.

Behavioral economists Hersh Shefrin and Meir Statman have noted how investors today take a similar approach to their different pools of assets.[2] Behavioral research has substantiated their observations. People actually do regard their financial assets as separate amounts they need for meeting different objectives. They keep "mental accounts" for separate needs.

What people don't do, it seems, is regard their financial assets as a single lump sum, even though much of standard finance theory (that is, theories that assume that all investors are rational) recommends they do just that, arguing that the consolidated approach is the most efficient, rational approach to take.

Building on the findings of behavioral finance, a number of theorists and practitioners have taken up the cause of goal-based investing as a way of managing behavioral biases as well as assuring basic lifestyle requirements at the same time.

Despite the behavioral bias implicit in "mental accounting," there is nothing dysfunctional or ultimately irrational about goal-based investing. Consider a recent brokerage statement that a friend of ours recently received. Because the tax law dictates separate treatment of retirement accounts, educational accounts, and taxable ones, the report our friend receives is broken out into three separate categories.

Each one of these categories actually corresponds to his goals: retirement, educational spending for his children, and his (taxable) reserve account for unanticipated emergencies. If he had no other investments (he does), then this report would provide him with good information on his progress toward each of his goals. It could, under certain circumstances, make good sense to manage each one of these accounts separately from the others.

On the other hand, imagine that our friend had received a different report—one that segregated his accounts based on the *sources*, not the uses, of his money. Believe it or not, this does happen when people delay decision-making. Suppose, too, that he managed each of these accounts separately— again, this is not an uncommon behavior pattern. There might be one account from a rollover retirement account at a former employer and a separate one composed of his recent IRA contributions. Despite their different funding sources, these two accounts are both retirement accounts, and there's no justifiable reason to manage them separately. Finally, imagine that he had never done anything about a small bequest from his late grandfather—again, not uncommon. As a result, his years-old inheritance would be parked in yet another account—a taxable one, kept separate, and managed separately from the rest.

There is no good reason for keeping separate jars of money based on who gave you the money in the first place. The separate accounts in this imaginary example are entirely dysfunctional. They serve no purpose. All they accomplish is confusing—and probably paralyzing—the investor.

The takeaway is that investor biases, as identified by Behavioral Finance, and good advice are not by definition incompatible. It's the end point of the advice that makes the difference.

Summing Up

To close, let's see how the matching approach, with its joint emphasis on personal goals and human capital, solves some key shortcomings of conventional investment advice.

Sam wants to know what's new about Paul's methods. He has talked at length with his tax advisor and believes that many of Paul's initial questions appear quite orthodox. In a typical consultation, it would be common for a financial advisor to spend time getting to know the client, often with the help of a questionnaire, and to ask about financial aspirations and goals. Questions would cover such topics as annual income, plans for retiring, and any pension income that might be expected.

In an early consultation, it would be typical, too, for an advisor to look at spending patterns and review the client's overall financial position, including all account balances. It's also common for advisors to use a separate questionnaire to help judge the client's attitude toward risk.

But in addition to all these practices, Paul also does something unusual: He takes special note of a person's career plans and lifelong income expectations. As we've seen, most conventional advisors don't generally pursue the human capital subplot much beyond asking about current income and later retirement plans. This leaves an important gap in their understanding of an investor's capacity for saving—and risk—at different stages of life.

Julia, too, wants more clarification from Paul about his approach. She's been told to be on the lookout for an investment policy statement. That sounds important and serious to her, and she is wondering whether they will be covering it in their meetings. She has not heard it mentioned so far.

The short answer to her question is yes: They will each develop a personal investment policy statement. But it will be an investment policy statement with a twist. It will start with investor goals, distinguish wants from needs, and use earnings expectations to create a lifetime budget and a safe investment zone to protect those basic needs.

Next, as we'll see in Part II, it will add the element of each investor's risk capacity—based largely on human capital—to make sure that the safe investment zone is the right size and that the implied risk set point corresponds to the investor's objective ability to take risk.

By contrast, a traditional investment policy statement takes many of the same ingredients but bakes them into a very different pie. It uses the client's goals, risk tolerance, and ability to take risk, although these risk measures usually go only lightly over human capital and are admittedly vague. Then the policy statement typically jumps to the return required to achieve the investor's goals.

This return requirement is generally calculated by working backward. Essentially, it's what you'd need to earn to achieve your specified outcomes in light of an expected savings rate and time line.

The required return is typically then blended with an appraisal of the investor's risk profile. Investors are commonly labeled as conservative, neutral, or aggressive, based largely on their answers to questionnaires. These blunt tools are used to tweak the required rate of return to arrive at a final allocation—usually putting 50, 60 or 70 percent into equities. In this way, the risk-adjusted required return typically becomes paramount in shaping an investor's portfolio. Higher required returns are biased toward higher equity allocations.

Compare this with the goal-based approach, which views the future in terms of spending and not in terms of a mechanical required rate of return or a magic number. It's geared instead to safeguard your basic needs. And, by setting needs apart from wants—and taking account of income expectations—it can also determine *how much* to put into safe, inflation-protected investments. If your needs are not attainable through safe instruments, the solution is not to increase the rate of return by upping the level of risk. Instead, goals may be revised, savings increased, or income boosted through added years of work.

Finding your risk set point is at the crux of the goal-based policy statement. Risky assets are not off-limits. But the amount you invest in risky assets is based on protecting your personal minimum baseline needs—and not on some preset formula or on maximizing investment returns. In the end, it's all about you and your destinations.

PART II

RISK MATTERS

CHAPTER 4

The Mismeasure of Risk

Look before you leap for as you sow, ye are like to reap.
—Samuel Butler

Financial risk is often cheered when it leads to large rewards but decried when it ends in failure. In this chapter and the next we'll address some of the cognitive dissonance that's so common on the subject of risk. We'll take special aim at one of the most deceptive refrains in the investment songbook—that stocks are safe in the long run—and we'll explain why it is so misleading. We'll also try to unmask some of the hidden snares that get in the way of good decisions.

To make these traps and distortions easier to remember, we'll give them alliterative tags: We'll talk about hype, hope, and hypothesis creep. The hype comes from overenthusiastic promotion. Hope is our undying talent for self-deception in pursuit of optimistic ends. And hypothesis creep is the stretching of accurate assertions into overstated palaver about the power of time to dissolve risk.

With a better appreciation of why we fail to assess risk properly, we'll be in a better position to self-correct. The idea is to build your confidence and expedite good risk decisions once you are ready to fine-tune your investment plan.

Defining Risk

To start, we need to define what we mean by risk. To build your own insight, ask yourself what risk means to you, based on your own exposures to risks—financial or otherwise. A few proposed definitions of risk that commonly surface include: the unknown; the chance that something harmful may happen; uncertain outcomes that may cause loss; and uncertainty that arouses fear.

Let's discard the idea that risk is nothing but the unknown, because risk is more than the ordinary uncertainty that surrounds our lives. By referring to harm, loss, and fear, the next three suggestions reflect one fundamental property of risk: Somebody has to *care* about the consequences if uncertainty is to be understood as risk.

The notion of "caring" or "mattering" is central. It captures both the potential (objective) *impact* of uncertainty as well as its (subjective) *bite*. This brings us close to the definition we'll adopt: *Investment risk is uncertainty that matters.* There are two prongs to this definition—the uncertainty, and what matters about it—and both are significant.

So, beyond the *odds* of hitting a rough patch, there are the *consequences* of loss to consider. What will happen if you miss your goals? If you look to your goals as benchmarks for measuring risk, you'll deepen your appreciation of what goals make sense for you.

Sleeping Tigers

Even though goal-based investing is on the rise, you'll still be swimming against the tides of convention. When it comes to investing, we've been well trained to believe that stocks are safe when held for a long time. Most investors were lulled into believing the story much too faithfully. And when the market plunged in the fall of 2008, it took even experts by surprise.

Investment professional Stacy Schaus has written deftly about how the unexpected volatility of 2008 affected her. As the markets spun down, she felt risk turn from an abstraction into a gut-wrenching ordeal. Her reaction was so intensely visceral that it reminded her of a similarly physical "frisson of fear" she'd experienced once before—on a visit to the Tiger Palace in Thailand.

There she faced a very long wait to see the tigers, so she paid extra to move to a shorter queue. It took her a while to realize that this new line—to photograph the animals— would send her inside with the tigers.

The new line moved fast. Before she could collect her thoughts, she found herself inside the pen—with a 350-pound tiger lolling its head on her lap. The tiger, though sleepy, was very real, and Stacy felt her heart "race with fear" as she concentrated on posing and smiling for photographs. (You can see some of the snapshots in her book.)

Meanwhile, Stacy's husband, also posing for photographs nearby, stood crouched and ready for flight behind a second tiger. His tiger was wide awake—and, to Stacy's eye, very hungry as it lustily licked its chops. Watching her husband, she felt her heart race and her stomach churn all over again, sensing the real danger of the situation. Luckily, the photo session ended as quickly as it had begun, with no harm done.

Schaus shared this story in her book about retirement plans because it reminded her so closely of the fear she felt during the "wild stock fluctuations" of 2008. Her candid description is hard to forget:

> . . . I am sure that I am not alone. Suddenly, I found that the amount of risk I was taking in my retirement accounts was more than I was comfortable with taking. It was as if I had been sitting with a sleeping tiger in

my lap, which had now awoken. . . . As we watched the
global financial markets sputter and lurch, I was aston-
ished that I could have taken on so much risk. What
had I been thinking?[1]

Like many Americans, Schaus experienced loss in all
her assets at once—her family's savings for their children's
college education, the value of their home, household savings, and retirement accounts. A consistent, prudent, long-
term saver and investor, she had been lured into taking
much more risk than she wanted.

Schaus vowed to return to a better risk balance once the
storm cleared.

As Schaus suggested, she was certainly not alone. Risky
investments have been a source of anxiety for many people
in the wake of the 2008 shock. Decisions made with equa-
nimity when the market was on the way up now seem impos-
sibly risky—as they do for Sam, Julia, Patrick, and Sue, who
keep voicing their many regrets.

They want a less dangerous answer.

The Lure of Hype

But how do you find the right risk balance that should be
every investor's Holy Grail? The solution starts with an
adjustment of flawed risk perceptions. It's helpful to see
through the many distortions that are regularly pitched our
way to champion high-risk investment products. Promotion
can be powerful—and, when it is persistent or clever, it can
breed familiarity or even trust.

Advocacy campaigns have played a big role in fostering
public comfort with stock ownership without a commen-
surate understanding of the risk that is involved. To get a
sense of their great influence, try surveying the so-called
educational content provided by investment industry sponsors, the financial media—and even government regulators
in the financial realm.

This is the tack that Paul took. He handed each participant a different list of web sites and educational material to cover, asking them to pay attention to the depiction of risk. What are the messages about risk–reward trade-offs that stick? How does the advice align with the definition of risk we've just adopted? They would report back on what they learned.

As background for their reading, Paul gave them a glossary of key investment terms, which you'll find in this chapter.

The precepts they encountered turned out to be familiar adages: Buy stocks to ensure you achieve the return you need on your investments. Diversify, and hold your stocks for a long time—more than 10 years, and preferably for 15 years or more. Market statistics, and history, demonstrate that timidity does not pay—over a span of 15 years, owning stocks is always better than owning short-term government bonds.[2]

There was no news here. The material they reviewed was well summarized in Nobelist Paul Samuelson's 1994 article about the "Long-Term Case for Equities and How It Can Be Oversold."[3] Even the investor education provided by government agencies such as the Securities and Exchange Commission—which you might expect to be impartial and science-based—presented a similar pitch.

It was an old story, but it was not dull. Sam landed an interactive drill that fascinated him once he started playing with it. He was asked to sample and review a few web-based financial wizards that claim to come up with a "personal" retirement portfolio tailored to your risk. You can try this, too, by googling "asset allocation calculator" and jumping right in.

The Time Diversification Fallacy

Sam found the "wizards" quite similar. Each asked a few simple questions in order to set some narrow parameters: age (or investment horizon, or years until retirement) and risk tolerance. Some added more whistles and bells, such as the amount of money desired and the amount of money available to invest. But all were simple and brief, meant as quick guides.

Most of the interactive calculators gave Sam the opportunity to rein in risk according to his personal preferences. They asked about his risk tolerance—he could choose small, medium, or large, or he could opt for none. Typically, they followed with a question about his flexibility in missing his goal—was it great, small, or nonexistent?

Sam made sure to set his risk tolerance to zero. Try as he might, and as much as he insisted that he wanted to take no risk, he kept getting a portfolio with 60 percent invested in stocks as long as his time horizon exceeded 15 years. It was only when he shortened the time line to 10 years that the stock allocation fell—but only by a little, to 50 or 55 percent. When he reduced his time horizon down to 3 to 5 years, he got a much smaller stock allocation, but it still came in at 25 percent.

In other words, the algorithms behind the wizards placed nearly all their weight on time horizon. Even a zero risk tolerance translated into a portfolio leaning 60-40 toward stocks. Time, if you are to believe the wizards, cures all ills.

Some Basic Definitions

Assets: An asset is anything that has economic value.

Financial Markets: The basic types of financial assets are debt, equity, and derivatives.

Equity: Equity is the claim of a firm's owners. Equity securities are called stocks.

Stocks: A common stock is a share of a company's assets and earnings. This means that a stockholder, or shareholder, owns a part of the company. Stockholders are entitled to receive dividends issued by the corporation and usually have voting rights.

Debt Instruments: These are issued by borrowers and are also called "fixed-income" instruments because they promise to pay fixed amounts of money over time. They include government and corporate bonds, residential and commercial mortgages, and consumer loans.

Inflation-Protected Bonds: Bonds that have their interest and principal denominated in terms of the purchasing power of a basket of goods and services in a particular country. The United States began issuing such bonds in 1997. In 1998, it added inflation protected savings bonds. *These are called Treasury Inflation Protected Securities (TIPS) and I Bonds, respectively.* The interest rate is a risk-free real rate.

Money Market: The market for short-term debt is called the "money market." It includes debt instruments with a maturity of *less than one year.* Money markets are *liquid*: that is, money-market instruments can be converted into *cash* with relative ease, speed, and low cost.

Derivatives (most commonly options and forward contracts): Financial instruments that derive their value from the prices of one or more underlying assets. (We'll postpone talking about these for now.)

The Standard & Poor's 500 Index (the S&P 500): An index representing the value of a basket of the 500 largest (and widely held) U.S. companies. The index is an average, with each company in it weighted by its market valuation. The index is often used as a surrogate for the broad stock market.

The idea that time erases risk is so prevalent, and so wrong, that we will devote a large part of the next chapter to it. For now, let's summarize by saying that the argument for time diversification is based on a mangled version of a more rigorously correct statement. But it is mathematically incorrect. As we've seen, the chances of loss do decline over time, but this hardly means that the odds are zero, or negligible, just because the horizon is long.[4]

Sam, who was settling happily into his newfound role as in-house skeptic, noted an additional flaw, which harkened back to the basic definition of risk. To evaluate risk, you need to know more than just the odds of loss. You also need to appreciate the effects of losing. Yet these allocation calculators had little or nothing to say about the magnitude of potential losses. They were silent about investor goals and the *consequences* of missing them.[5]

Sam is onto something. In fact, even though the *odds* of loss do fall over long periods, the *size* of potential losses gets larger, not smaller, over time.

The Illusion of Stocks as an Inflation Shield

Julia was asked to look at a few investor education web sites. Primed now to detect promotion when she saw it, she'd been surprised to find equity advocacy even on the government-sponsored sites. She was especially struck by a video clip from the educational platform on the web site of the Financial Industry Regulatory Authority (FINRA), an independent industry self-regulatory organization.

The film depicted a young, good-looking couple preparing dinner together in their well-appointed kitchen— a scene she found easy to relate to. They were exchanging opinions about where they should be investing. Husband and wife were plainly ordinary, prudent people and not greedy high rollers. Still, the wife informed her husband that it was *too risky* for them *not* to be in stocks.

Otherwise, she said, they stood to be snookered by inflation. Bank CDs might seem safe because they are insured (up to a maximum principal amount). But bank CDs and other cash investments couldn't possibly keep pace with inflation should it arise and surprise. Ergo, the timid choice is actually the riskier choice. Message: Don't be timid. Don't simply exchange inflation risk for market risk. Choose stocks.

Is this a principle you've been trained to believe? Julia confessed that the video looked convincing. It came from a reliable source while sounding comfortably familiar. She knew that cash in the bank was vulnerable to inflation because the

interest could easily be outmatched by inflation, leaving her
with less purchasing power than she had started out with.

Yet she sensed that the pitch flew in the face of her own
recent experience. Her stock portfolio had not kept up with
inflation. She was unsure of what to think.

The claim that only equities can protect you against
inflation is a perennial chestnut of conventional wisdom.
The video Julia watched was not an obscure footnote buried
in a dusty journal—it was a refrain that recurred in most of
the "educational" web sites she looked at.

How wonderful if stock market returns turn out to protect owners against inflation. The notion even has intuitive
appeal, because businesses are seen as able to dodge inflation by raising prices—and stocks are ownership shares of
those same companies.

The truth, though, is less reassuring. Firms can't invariably
exercise pricing power—not by a long shot. And the actual evidence of a close relationship between stock returns and inflation is nowhere to be had. The best that can be said is that the
data are indeterminate. There is almost no evidence at all that
stocks can provide immediate protection against long-term
inflation, and even some evidence to the contrary. The fact
that inflation rates differ around the globe further muddies
the picture.

Oddly, the seductive video Julia had watched made no
mention of other instruments that actually do provide inflation protection. It had set up a false either-or comparison
between stocks and the money market—or short-term cashlike
investments—which are very vulnerable to real losses through
inflation. But the video (along with scores of other teaching
tools on- and off-line) made no mention of TIPS and I Bonds—
U.S. government-guaranteed, inflation-linked investments.

It's a pitch that is psychologically seductive. But there
are two important errors here—one apiece of commission
and omission—that are worth paying attention to because
they so distort the perception of the real risk of stocks.

Deceptions of Target-Date Funds

Patrick's charge was to survey so-called "target-date" funds and to assess their risk. These funds are designed to make investing simple by reducing their level of investment risk over time. Participants choose a date as close as possible to their planned retirement. The funds start out in riskier investments, in search of higher returns. Gradually, as the target date approaches, they shift their holdings into lower-risk assets.

Based on their name, Patrick had assumed that the target-date funds in his employer's 401(k) retirement plan promised safety in the form of a known amount when they "matured." That's why he felt comfortable dividing his retirement portfolio between a target-date fund and a rather risky technology fund. He'd expected his target-date funds to provide ballast.

Yet in 2008, the year that the S&P 500 (the index of the largest 500 U.S. public companies) fell 41 percent, his investment also fell considerably. His research showed him that the average target-date fund with a 2010 target lost 24 percent of its value, and at least one 2010 target-date fund fell by 41 percent. This happened within 2 short years of their supposed target date.

He'd been wrong. This was not a safe investment. There were no guarantees. Patrick found the name of the investment the cruelest deception—a bold case of untruth in labeling.

But he learned other things that also disturbed him. He found the funds' objectives and practices hard to ferret out, and he discovered considerable variation among different fund families. And he realized that many of them used different ways to describe and measure risk. "What a mess," he told Paul and company.

Sue reacted to Patrick's discussion with disappointment. The neat thing she'd expected from these funds was how well they might fit into the model they'd begun to build. She'd thought that these investments, with their target dates, might actually be geared toward meeting investor goals by providing money matched to investors' dates and needs.

This might have been the case if the funds had promised a specific amount, or even a specific range, at the target date. Instead, they appeared to be yet one more way for an investor to take on risk without realizing it.

For those who share Sue's disappointment, this is a call to engagement. With the growing number of retirements about to burgeon in America, investment firms are on the case. Market reception will make a difference. The more the public demands transparency and standardization of risk measurements, the more likely we are to get some better investment products—both for retirees and for people still saving for retirement.

How We Learned to Stop Worrying and Love the Market

The message to emerge from all this hype has been inescapable: In the long run, the stock market can only go up. Its ascent is inexorable and predictable. Long-term stock returns are seen as near certain while risks appear minimal, and only temporary.

And the messaging has been effective: The familiar market propositions come across as bedrock fact. For the most part, the public views them as scientific truth, although this is hardly the case.

It may surprise you, but all this confidence is rather new. Prevailing attitudes and behavior before the early 1980s were different. Fewer people owned stocks then, and the general popular attitude to buying stocks was wariness, not ebullience or complacency.

This is an irony that Julia, recalling her elderly parents and her late aunt, knows well. They avoided stocks like the plague, and Julia has often remarked on the much bolder attitudes that are now common in her generation.

She'd assumed that her parents were living with the outdated legacy of the Depression. Plus, she thought, they had a modest pension that they'd always relied on. These days, few people Julia's age had pensions like that.

Julia has reasoned that she differs from her parents on many other subjects too—often based on better science and newer information. Take health, for example, or nutrition and exercise. "Why is the change in risk perception not progress toward accuracy and self-betterment?" she wants to know.

Unfortunately, the American public's embrace of stocks is not at all related to the spread of sound knowledge. It's useful to consider how the transition actually evolved—because the real story resists a triumphalist interpretation.

Let's look at a few of the key plot lines. Far from signaling the march of scientific progress, the taming of investor perceptions traces back primarily to the gradual shift in pension fund arrangements since the 1970s and early 1980s. That's when a steady evolution began away from so-called defined benefit plans and toward so-called defined contribution plans instead. In particular, the tax-deferred 401(k) came into being, almost accidentally, in 1980.

Pensions Shift Shape

The new pension funding arrangements offered some innovations and advantages. Defined benefit pensions only rarely protect beneficiaries against inflation, and the opportunity for inflation-protected return does exist in defined-contribution plans, at least in theory if not practice. Also, by now, most defined-contribution plans offer participants a great deal of choice, as well as improved portability.

Over time, defined contribution plans have come to eclipse traditional pension plans. An important upshot of this trend has been that the risk, as well as the task, of funding retirement has moved from employer to employee.

It's hard to overemphasize the importance of this transformation to the way Americans invest today.

The great pension makeover set a retail investment boomlet in motion. It pulled billions of dollars into mutual funds and the stock market. To get an idea of how explo-sive the expansion has been, consider that in 1984 there were 459 equity mutual funds in the United States. By 2008, there were 4,830—and they held about $3.75 trillion.

Most people don't realize that 401(k) plans were origi-nally intended as a *supplement* to defined benefit pensions. It made some sense for their owners then to take higher risk in search of higher investment returns, because the basics were largely assured.

If you recall how we distinguished needs, or essentials, from wants, or extras, then it's easy to see that the 401(k)s started out as vehicles to fund the aspirational goals. For the workers and employees who had them, traditional pensions covered basic needs.

Today, though, 401(k)s are no longer supplements to defined benefit plans. They must provide for basic needs and not just aspirational goals. As a result, the amount of risk a 401(k) investor can afford to take is much smaller.

With the incentive of tax deferral, other retirement sav-ings plans have also grown in scale and availability—including plans for the self-employed, plans for nonprofit and govern-ment employees, and more. They are not restricted to equity investments, but the message from the retirement planning world has emphasized stocks and stock mutual funds as the core of a "sensible" long-term investing strategy.

And the word is out. In the 1970s, stock ownership (including mutual funds) was limited to about one in four or five American households. By 2008, nearly half of American households owned stock. Equity ownership peaked at about 53 percent just before the market decline of 2001. Stock own-ership did taper off in the wake of market turbulence, but not by much.

The problem is that this message comes with all the distor-tions we've been discussing. Unbiased, factual information— free of selective omission—is not easy to come by, as you've seen from our quick excursion into online investor education.

The Seductions of a Long Bull Market

If stocks had remained in the doldrums or in decline, the surge in their popularity may never have happened. In tandem with the redrawing of the retirement pension map, though, the U.S. stock market began to soar. In 1983, the S&P index took off on a steady climb that continued more or less without a hitch until a sudden and dramatic collapse took people by surprise in 1987.

The breakdown of October 1987 was quickly ironed out, partly through actions of the Federal Reserve. The S&P returned to its pre-crash level in less than a year. For the next 12 years, the market resumed its upward climb, taking only a few short breathers here and there until 2000.

In retrospect, the quick restoration of stock market value that followed the 1987 decline probably encouraged people to ignore market volatility as a message about risk. To the contrary, a self-sustaining pattern of opportunistic "buying on the dips" developed. The common view at that time held that the slumps would be short-lived—and so they appeared.

The run-up of stock prices in the 1980s and especially the 1990s promoted a self-reinforcing faith in equities as the road to sure riches—and the availability of 401(k) and IRA investment options provided added opportunity. Many individuals who might not otherwise have found the means to buy stocks or stock mutual funds were able to do so easily—by using the savings in their retirement accounts, which often included matching contributions from employers.

It's hard to underestimate the persuasive power of the long bull market. Earlier generations had been warned off stocks following the collapses of the post-Roaring Twenties Depression—and in the post–Go-Go Sixties market decline of the 1970s.

The late-20th-century bull market ran long and strong enough to convince a massive following of its enduring profitability. An entire cohort of Baby Boomers was educated at its knee. Even if the ascent got interrupted from time to time, it seemed as though it could not end.

But the market's nearly steady upward run was masking the true inherent risk.

The Internet Accelerates a Trend

The growing appetite for stock ownership found further encouragement in another new trend—one that traced its early origins back to 1979—the buying and selling of securities online by consumers, without ever talking to a broker. The rise of personal computing and the Internet brought well known changes to consumer stock trading.

The investment industry took advantage of new cyber opportunities, offering a widening array of trading, portfolio management, and research tools online. A retail financial supermarket—a notion dreamed up more than 30 years ago—became a thriving reality. To this chorus of champions, the media also lent its voice, through a few dedicated financial cable networks, cheerleading financial web sites, and more.

Expansionary growth cycled faster and bigger in the decade of the 1990s, eventually fueling a speculative investment trend that culminated in the dot-com bubble—a mania that eventually imploded, bringing with it a recession and considerable pain.

Lessons were learned. But the principal cautionary message seemed narrow. It focused on the real dangers of rapid stock churning and the popular practice of "day-trading" individual stocks by amateurs at home. The experts reserved their sharpest barbs for speculative companies (who deserved the criticism).

Critiques of the excessive enthusiasm for the market as a whole were far fewer, although a few important exceptions stand out. By and large, the inherent riskiness of stocks outside the technology sector escaped widespread and fundamental scrutiny.

The numbers bear this out. Despite the market's decline in 2001 and 2002, individual investors continued until the end of 2004 to express great confidence that it would rebound within the coming year. The confidence index then, according to the data collected by the Yale School of Management, stood at a remarkable 95.62 percent. Confidence levels fell in 2005 and 2006, but not below the 80 percent mark.

Thanks to skillful percent proselytizing and the memory of the market's long bull run, people continued to underrate risk. Against the evidence and against the science, the flawed conventional theories endured. It would take one more market collapse in the space of just a few years—and a bone-cracking one at that—to spur a reassessment.

Yet—despite a flood of regret and re-evaluation, and a newfound interest in understanding risk—the beat goes on.[6]

CHAPTER

The Allure of Hope

Our minds are not built…to work by the rules of
probability, though these rules clearly govern our universe.
　　　　　　　　　　　　　　　　　—Stephen Jay Gould

T he credo of stocks-for-the-long-term owes its currency not just to outside influence but also to our cognitive makeup. We have been willing collaborators in deception. Emotion biases our perceptions, coaxing us to take the bait at nearly every turn.

We humans are simply not wired well for judging risk.

Behavioral economists have amply demonstrated these cognitive failings in recent years—and, as we discuss a few of them, you are likely to recognize them immediately, even if you've never heard of them before. (In fact, one of the early and most recognized pioneers of the field, the late psychologist Amos Tversky, once modestly demurred that all he had done was to employ scientific methods to examine behaviors that were well known to advertisers and used-car salesmen.[1]) Still, behavioral economists have done us a service by bringing the subject to the fore, encouraging us all to recognize the flaws in our ability to make decisions under uncertainty.

As we're learning from psychology and neuroscience research, the human mind draws on two disparate ways of knowing. There is the part of us that intuits and the part that reasons. The two operating systems don't always work in concert. The intuitive brain is ruled by habit and emotion—and it tends to resist change. It regularly uses shortcuts to arrive at quick conclusions. When its perceptions differ from the conclusions of the rational brain, it is the emotional side that prevails, more often than not.

We are all literally of two minds, and our feelings usually win.

Too Much Confidence

This bifurcation is relevant to the way we tend to judge risk—intuitively, rather than via technical or rational measurements. So, as Stacy Schaus's tiger story illustrates, we tend to notice risk primarily when it stirs our emotions.

But when things are going well, investors typically exhibit overconfidence about their prospects. The undue confidence in their own abilities leads them to underplay (or ignore) the risks that they are taking.

Excessive optimism helps explain the popularity of the stocks-for-the-long-run doctrine. The pseudo-factual statement that stocks always succeed in the long run provides an overconfident investor with more grist for the optimistic mill. To understand how easily investors slide into overconfident patterns, it's worth knowing how common overconfident behavior is in general. Research has shown, for example, that people tend to rank themselves above-average on just about all favorable traits. Overconfidence extends beyond investment skill to driving ability, a sense of humor, and even expected longevity. In one often-cited example, when American students were asked to rate their own driving safety, more than three-fourths believed they were in the top third of the group.

Overconfidence may get cultural reinforcement too—an international comparison of the math achievement of young pupils around the world placed U.S. students below the 10 highest-scoring countries, yet the same American youngsters ranked near the top on their confidence in their ability to do math.

You may recognize this as the Lake Wobegon effect, where, as Garrison Keillor's satire would have it, "the women are strong, the men are good looking and all the children are above average."

Common as it is, overconfidence is not universal. There is evidence, for example, that women are less confident—and more risk averse—in their investment behavior than men. This difference probably holds in other realms as well—at least one study, for instance, has shown that women underestimate their own intelligence scores whereas men consistently overestimate theirs.

This is a caveat that is important for Sue and Julia to hear, because neither is pleased to learn about overconfidence as typical investor behavior. It rings no bells for either of them.

As an entrepreneur and business owner, Julia embraces her confidence, even if it tilts occasionally to excess. She relies on it for success. Sue objects too, but for different reasons. Since her divorce, she shrinks from any argument aimed at cutting her confidence to size.

It's worth emphasizing, then, that confidence differs from optimistic overconfidence. Psychologist Daniel Kahneman—Amos Tversky's longtime collaborator and the winner of the 2002 Nobel Prize in Economics—has affirmed this central distinction. Speaking with the editors of Forbes. com in 2002, Kahneman explained:

> When you are making a decision whether or not to go
> for something," he said, "my guess is that knowing the

odds won't hurt you, if you're brave. But when you are executing, not to be asking yourself at every moment in time whether you will succeed or not is certainly a good thing. . . . In many cases, what looks like risk-taking is not courage at all, it's just unrealistic optimism. Courage is willingness to take the risk once you know the odds. Optimistic overconfidence means you are taking the risk because you don't know the odds. It's a big difference.[2]

Optimism can be a great motivator. It helps especially when it comes to implementing plans. Although optimism is healthy, however, it's not always appropriate. You would not want rose-colored glasses in a financial advisor, for instance.

The Illusion of Control

Overconfident or not, almost everyone can recognize some aspects of themselves in a cluster of related behaviors. These habits are so common that they don't stand out, yet they subtly subvert our ability to assess risk. By learning to spot them in action, we can start to break their hold.

First, there is the confidence that flows from a sense of control—whether real or imagined. Abundant evidence suggests that people do feel more secure when they believe they are in control—even when they plainly are not. There are travelers, for example, who fear flying, although they're quite comfortable behind the wheel of a car. Statistically, they have it backwards—the odds of serious mishap on the highway greatly outweigh the risks of air travel. But on the road, they occupy the driver's seat, and that seems to make all the psychological difference. The common global phenomenon of driver overconfidence may similarly stem from the illusion of control.

The problem is that illusions of control bring a false sense of mastery over risk.

In another example of the illusion of control and its consequences, participants in a coin-tossing experiment bet more money when given the chance to call heads or tails *before* the coin was tossed than *after*. Apparently, calling the coin after it had been tossed exposed the entirely speculative nature of the game, while choosing the call in advance imparted an illusion of influence over the result.

Researchers report similar patterns among buyers of lottery tickets. Buyers strongly prefer to choose the number they're betting to match, rather than passively accepting a computer-generated number. Active involvement gives them a sense of empowerment against the odds—even though the control is illusory.

An illusion of information can feel equally aggrandizing. The fault here may lie deep in the human brain. More than we realize, we rely on context for most of our perceptions—of size, for example, or loudness, or distance. If you are seated in a dark room, looking at a bright object, with no clues about how close or far away that object actually is, it's impossible to make a good judgment about its size.

Lacking the necessary information, though, our minds will jump to conclusions and deliver a clear impression— one that appears incontrovertibly true. In the absence of necessary information, the brain seems to reflexively fill in the gaps with its own interpretation.

The trouble is that we can't distinguish between factual evidence and manufactured shortcuts to interpretation. Turn the lights back on, and you may be amazed that the bright object is far smaller and farther away (or larger and closer) than you had imagined. Gather the outcomes of your one-time financial bets, and with 20/20 hindsight you may learn how skewed your assumptions were.

Illusions of information and control can lead to magical thinking. The gamblers who favored coin-tosses they could call in advance are a prime example. So, too, are investors who were gulled into fraudulent Ponzi schemes with mammoth expectations. The same can be said about the many other investors who planned to save little but reap bounteously, based on prospects of supersized returns.

Some psychologists have theorized that magical or wishful thinking is a protective cloak that people slip into when confronting complex matters that seem beyond their comprehension. In this view, the uncontrollable and the unknowable generate so much frustration, helplessness, and even anger that many people invoke fantasy as a way to limit the pain. Either way—as reflexive interpretation or protective distraction—wishful thinking vastly undermines rational decision-making in uncertain situations.

Framing

We are also vulnerable to the way things are presented to us. Our susceptibility to framing makes us easy to manipulate and is another wellspring for overconfidence, illusory knowledge, and flawed estimation of risk.

As Madison Avenue has long understood, framing and innuendo have great unconscious power to shape our attitudes and actions. It's well known that vendors can fool consumers with their choice of words. To extract extra fees from credit cardholders—without angering or losing them—banks often shun explicit fees but provide inferior options at a so-called discount instead. What they're offering is exactly the same, but customers don't leave.

In a similar vein, individuals display illogical preferences, depending on whether there is a subpar option available to them or not. In one well known study, people were offered either a set amount of cash or a luxury Cross pen of equal value. Only a third of them chose the pen. But if their available choices were widened to include the Cross pen, the same set amount of cash, and an inferior pen as well, far more people—nearly half—chose the Cross pen. When comparisons are offered, things can be made to look suddenly good.

Framing comes into play in surprising ways. Another well known inconsistency that almost all of us display is to apply a different yardstick depending on whether we are an outsider or an insider. If you've read through our various illustrations of illogical behavior but dismissed them as characterizing "other people" and not you, maybe it's time to think again. Difficult as it may be, try rereading them in the first person singular, and listen for resonance.

Framing exerts potent influence on the perception of risk, especially when it comes to weighing losses and gains. People hate to lose even more than they like to win—this is a central conclusion of Tversky and Kahneman's work—and they act differently, depending on whether they are presented with the prospect of a sure gain or certain loss. When offered a choice between a sure gain and the possibility of an equal loss, people overwhelmingly avoid risk and stick with the sure gain.[3]

Interestingly, though, this behavior reverses when the choice is between a certain *loss* and a possible gain. To avoid the sure loss, most people now become willing to take risks they would otherwise shun. Thus, in order to avoid losing $100 for sure, they become irrationally willing to risk losing much more than $100—in exchange for the (small) chance they may end up losing nothing.

Losses can be insidious, in other words, because they summon emotions rather than reason in their wake. Loss can, and regularly does, induce people to throw good money after bad in hopes of recovering what they once had—and consider rightly theirs. If, however, the same risky investment is framed outside the individual's prior loss, chances are that he or she will reconsider and act more rationally.

Sue in particular recognizes the odd nexus between losses and a willingness to take more risk. Lately, following her divorce settlement, she's been highly conscious of her diminished means. In talking with her peers, she's aware that she's still angry with her ex-husband for taking too much risk in their original portfolio and losing so much money.

Sue has realized that her raw feelings have made her susceptible to large swings in the way she regards risk—dismissively on some days and with great concern on others. In fact, as a way of making up some of her losses, she had been considering an early-stage investment in a company where she knows the principals and expects especially high returns. She'd felt that her inside knowledge would ensure success. Now she's not so sure. For the moment, the group's conversation about human behavior is reinforcing her wary side. She is going to sort out her plans only after learning more.

Sam, on the other hand, has already been persuaded by his long layoff that he needs to be wary of risk. He joined the group, after all, because he was so shaken by how fast his savings had dwindled.

He emphatically wants to avoid losing more money than he can afford. He recognizes himself in the description of overconfidence. He recalls how he loaded up on technology stocks in the late 1990s and for a long time after that. He works in the technology industry, and had always reckoned that his expertise would guide him through the shoals.

On the other hand, by listening to Paul and comparing himself to the other group members, Sam realizes that his large store of potential income from work gives him latitude. He's beginning to believe that he may have overreacted like a yo-yo. After taking too much risk, he wonders whether he's becoming much too defensive. His solution is not going to be risk avoidance, he understands, but risk calibration.

Julia doesn't identify much with any of these descriptions at first, until she realizes how emotional she still is about her inheritance—to the point of paralysis. It's almost as though doing nothing is giving her an illusion of control—a kind of status quo confidence that she realizes is foolish but can't seem to shake.

With his background in psychology, Patrick has been naturally attracted to hearing about behavioral finance—and he wants to read up on the subject. But Patrick also fits the descriptions of an overconfident investor. He had enjoyed the thrills of day trading before the end of the Internet stock bubble—and is still very ambivalent about the inherent risk of the stock market.

It's useful to reflect on your own perceptions about risk. Do you recognize yourself in any of the behaviorists' portraits? Have hype and the overoptimistic allure of hope colored your reflexive assumptions about investment risk?

Probability Blindness

As we've noted, the popular perception of risk as benign in the long run also stems from another key cognitive shortcoming: probability blindness.

Thanks to probability blindness, the notion that risk fades with time remains stubbornly sticky. And yet, most of us know in our bones that uncertainty does not fade but rather builds over time. The weather is a good example. Which do you trust more—the 10-day prediction or tomorrow morning's report?

How can both these views be true?

Dueling Intuitions

To appreciate how automatically we expect risk to fan out over time, consider the hurricane cone.

From late May through November each year, tropical storms, hurricanes, and typhoons arrive dependably in the hurricane belt on either side of the equator. To warn the public about the likely path and vehemence of these gathering storms, meteorologists have developed precautionary pictures that map the storms' predicted track and intensity.

But predictions are imperfect, so forecasters typically draw a big teardrop-shaped perimeter around the expected route. This is the error zone. It represents a much larger area of potential landfall, usually a few hundred square miles. Called the cone of uncertainty (or the cone of danger), the area balloons outward, growing ever wider as the storm moves farther along its projected path and away from its most recent location.

The hurricane cone provides a more realistic warning than the projected track on its own. Consistent with the shape of the cone, the range of the deviations widens with distance and time.

As the storm moves forward, it will encounter increasing opportunities to change course—it may wobble, then accelerate, warm up, or slow down. Each prospective deviation opens up new possibilities. That's why the trajectory becomes less and less certain the more days we peer ahead. Only after the fact will the actual storm track be known.

The hurricane cone picture in Figure 5.1 registers immediately because it accords so well with common sense. In general, predictions inspire less and less confidence as they advance into the future.

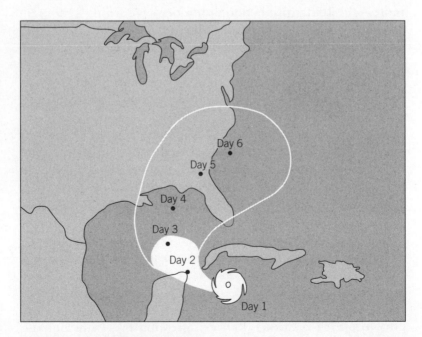

Figure 5.1   Uncertainty Grows over Time

This instinct about uncertainty dovetails with the related intuition that danger widens with exposure as time goes by. A person's lifetime risk of cancer is plainly greater than the risk of getting cancer before the age of 40. So, too, the risk that there will be a fatal airline crash over, say, the Andes, is higher over a 10-year period than in any single year. With growing exposure comes mounting risk.

Similarly, if your cousin Bob takes a shortcut as he walks home each day, cutting across a busy highway on his way, his risk of being hurt on any single crossing may not make your heart race—but over the course of the year, as the uncertainty grows, his odds of mishap increase. If you are a skilled parachutist who jumps, for fun, out of an airplane once a month, your accident risk is going to be greater over the coming year than on any one jump.

Over the long haul, the more you are exposed to danger, the more likely it is to catch up with you. The odds don't exactly add, but they do accumulate.

The cone of uncertainty model applies quite well to the way investments will perform over time. Here too, the span of possible outcomes widens as the time horizon lengthens.

Figure 5.2 shows how wide that range can grow in time. It represents a simplified 2-year investment. In each year there are only two possible outcomes—either the investment will increase by half or it will fall by one-quarter. Over time, the range of possible outcomes widens fast. In other words, the ending value of an investment is increasingly uncertain as the time horizon lengthens. Unavoidably, this greater dispersion of values over time means that severe losses (as well as gains) grow more likely.

Yet, overriding this instinctive understanding, the prevailing investment dogma has argued just the reverse. The creed that stocks grow steadily safer over time has managed to trump our common-sense assumption by appealing to a different set of homespun precepts.

Chief among these is a flawed surmise that, with the passage of time, downward fluctuations are balanced out by

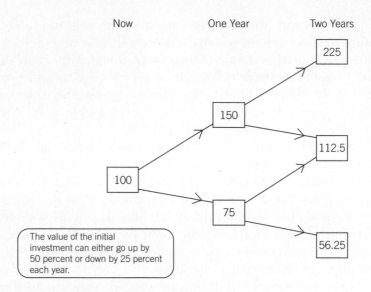

Now   One Year   Two Years

225

150

112.5

100

75

56.25

The value of the initial
investment can either go up by
50 percent or down by 25 percent
each year.

Figure 5.2   Investment Outcomes over Time

compensatory upward swings. Many people believe that each
step backward will be offset by more than one step forward.
The assumption is that you can own all the upside and none
of the downside just by sticking around.

Today's faith in stocks as a safe long-term investment
owes much of its traction to the best-selling book, *Stocks for
the Long Run,* by Wharton professor Jeremy Siegel, which first
appeared in 1994.[4] Siegel collected copious data reaching
back to 1802 and concluded that over long periods (possibly
17 years or more), stocks had beaten nominal government
bonds hands down. Far more than bonds, he said, stocks pos-
sessed the ability to preserve purchasing power over the long
run. And, over the long run, the short-run volatility of stocks
calmed down, providing investors with a secure investment
return.

As we've seen, Siegel's thesis has taken root—so much so
that it has become a near-foundational belief. And, as Sam
found when he played with automated allocation wizards, it is
hard to visit an educational web site without encountering it.

Part of the argument's allure is its optimism. We've already observed how emotion, promotion, and cognitive error can help pave the way for flawed perception. And, there is no question that Siegel's contentions about safety lost much of their nuance as they were recast into cereal-box slogans. Stocks were regularly presented as if they were as riskless over the long run as default-free government bonds. What a deal.

Some of Siegel's followers went to absurd extremes. In 1999, James K. Glassman and Kevin A. Hassett published the now infamously titled *Dow 36,000*.[5] (In 1999, the Dow Jones Industrial Average was fluctuating between 10,000 and 11,000.) Glassman and Hassett claimed that stocks were not very risky, and were therefore mispriced by people who believed they were. This widespread error presented a fabulous opportunity in their view. Once the rest of the market came to its senses and realized its mistake, the Dow would reach 36,000. Considering what has happened to the Dow Jones Industrial Average in the meantime, Dow 36,000 looks more than a little silly.

But Siegel's case has a serious core. Although we can dismiss some of its most extravagant distortions, we can't just leave it at that. We will also have to address the basic intuition that instills so much reflexive trust in its adherents—the presumption that the up-and-down fluctuations of the market cancel out *during any individual's long personal investment horizon*. Seen in this light, short-run riskiness melts into long-run safety—thus truly upending the cone-of-uncertainty intuition where we began.

It's urgent to resolve the contradiction. The safety of your investment goals depends on it.

The Perils of Probability

The stocks-for-the-long-run vision is based on some rigorously demonstrable truths about prospective returns and some highly misleading conclusions about risk. That's why we have characterized it as hypothesis creep—a garbled take on some basic perspectives from finance and mathematics.

The case relies heavily on the expectation that shortfalls will be overwhelmed by upward growth over time. Despite the accessibility of this intuition, it creates the false impression that a cycle of loss-offsetting gains is something anyone can capture simply by being patient.

But here's the rub. Stock returns are random. They resist close prediction. Even if long-run stock returns keep coming back to their own historical trend line, stock prices still move randomly. Proponents of stocks for the long run generally support this idea of so-called mean reversion, but even in this rendition, random noise buffets the annual returns in unexpected ways.

No one knows exactly what the path of stock returns will look like. There could be large swings or small, very long runs or extremely short ones. The path could include many above- or below-average years in a row. Mean reversion, if it happens at all, could be accomplished quickly or extremely slowly.

At bottom, it's inattention to the role of randomness that lets us unthinkingly harbor two dueling intuitions at once. When it comes to chance and luck, most of us wear dark blinkers.

Riddles of Randomness

A common device for touting the superiority of stocks in the long run is to chart historical U.S. stock returns over very long terms. Lengthy tables like these are used to show that over very long holding periods (of 60 to 100 years), the average inflation-adjusted return on stocks is quite steady, hovering around 6.5 percent.

Many people take assurance from these numbers. But they interpret the very long-run historical record much too narrowly, expecting to earn a real rate of return close to

7 percent—as long as they hold on for a while. When they subscribe, in principle, to the long-term nature of the engagement, they seldom reflect on how the long horizons fit their own circumstances.

But there are plenty of 20-year periods when U.S. stocks returned a lot less than 7 percent. The Great Depression is perhaps the most extreme example. An investor who bought stocks at their peak valuations before October 1929, and then held on, might not have lived long enough to find out. That investor would not even have recouped all losses, in real terms, until around 1950.

Even excluding the wild losses of the Great Depression, there are other instances when 20-year average annual returns fell below the returns on bonds—or even came close to zero. If you'd bought a broad stock index or its equivalent in 1965, it would have taken a full 18 years until you saw any positive real return. The inflation and market collapse of the 1970s were that severe.

At the end of 2010, the 20-year average annual real return of the broad stock market was closer to 4 per cent than to 7, and a year earlier it was lower still.

Or, consider Japan. In the 1980s, Japan was in the ascendant. Its car makers, electronics companies, and even its banks were seriously challenging their American rivals. Japanese property values were soaring. And the Japanese stock market was sky high after many years of extraordinary growth. In 1989, Japan's broad large-company stock index, the Nikkei 225, peaked at around 40,000. Today the Nikkei index is valued below 10,000. As Figure 5.3 shows, a Japanese retiree relying on the stock market in 1989 would have been even worse off than his U.S. counterpart in 1972.

Still, the promise of a continuous, steady return exerts a kind of magical charm. The assumption that the expected return will be one's own return is hard to resist. Partly this is because most people understand the lean years of the past as unique and nonrecurring—the results of either very high

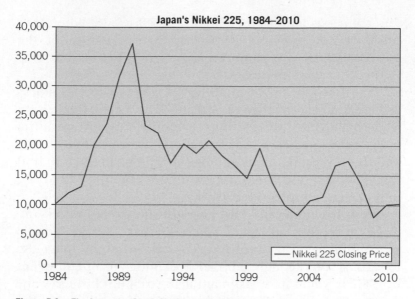

Figure 5.3   The Japanese Stock Market since 1984

inflation or the Great Depression. Partly, too, it's been the education of several decades that robust returns swallow up the bad years in the long term.

The social and cognitive traps we've just explored all play a role in promoting these perceptions, but the most serious among them is our probability blindness. Stock prices move randomly—and these views profoundly miss that central point. The conventional faith in stocks for the long run shows how resistant we are to grasping the way randomness rules our lives.

The issue is larger than ignorance, because experts, too, fall prey to confusion. As the scientist Stephen Jay Gould has put it, in his memorable essay about streaks in baseball and in life, "If we understood Lady Luck better, Las Vegas might still be a roadstop in the desert. . ."

Instead, we seem to respond well to narratives that impute predictable patterns to our investment returns. And the backstory—that losses are destined to be offset by larger gains—seems to provide a trusty rationale.

Patrick, you'll recall, was an extreme case, by his own admission. For a long time he was convinced that the stock market could only go up. Even when he lost money, he shrugged this off as a minor detour on a path that climbed only upward. He bought assiduously on the dips. Confident that he needed less to achieve more, he slashed his savings rate.

In fact, to hear him talk at the time—as he now half boasted and half rued—you might have thought his losses were rare. It was the big wins that he remembered, and he loved talking about them. Today, engulfed in bad news, he recognizes that his losses in the 1990s cut deeper into his and Marianne's wealth than he admitted at the time. But even today, much chastened by the market, he wants to believe that his balances will be restored if he remains faithful—because, he says, the long-term averages are due for a revival. He interprets the market's recent recovery as evidence.

Patrick has plenty of company. Our failure to comprehend probability has been the subject of several recent books, all studded with entertaining but disconcerting stories about how reliably we misunderstand the role of chance.

In a pertinent illustration, researchers recorded the sequence of a hundred actual coin tosses, and then inserted these results into a short list of made-up heads-and-tails sequences. They asked participants to find the one real sequence.

Few succeeded. People commonly expected the results to show balance. The odds, after all, are 50-50. But the truly random runs included long, imbalanced strings of successive heads (or tails).

Streaks in baseball and "hot hands" in basketball or cards provide vivid examples of the same tendency. Hot hands in basketball—along with hitting streaks in baseball— are widely accepted as true and well documented phenomena. As Stephen Jay Gould colorfully wrote, "You get that touch, build confidence; all nervousness fades, you find your rhythm; swish, swish, swish. Or you miss a few, get rattled, endure the booing, experience despair; hands start shaking and you realize that you shoulda stood in bed."[6]

The central conviction behind this belief is the premise that in normal play, scores and misses appear in virtually balanced succession. Long, uninterrupted runs appear to defy the odds—and are therefore best explained as personal acts of triumph, by athletes and fans alike.

Except that hot hands don't really exist, any more than streaks and slumps do in baseball, the stock market, or in life. Psychologist Amos Tversky, together with Thomas Gilovich and Robert Vallone, studied the entire play of the Philadelphia 76ers for over a season and discovered that the odds of a player's scoring a second basket did not rise after a successful basket. In addition, the number of successive baskets by any player—"runs" or "streaks"—was indistinguishable from the predictions of a random, coin-tossing model, where the odds of a score were the same for every shot.[7]

Of course, better players had better sequences—their overall odds of shooting a basket were better—but not beyond what could be predicted by the random probability model in light of their overall past performance.

There are clear parallels with stock investing. Like athletes, stocks tend to perform over time at their long-term average levels. In the case of stocks, we don't really know this number with precision because the methods of calculating it vary and can be unreliable. But let's assume that it's just below 7 percent. That does *not* mean that every stockholder is going to earn an average of 7 percent.

It would be as wrong to expect a smooth and predictable performance from stocks as from basketball players. A stock's returns actually have a longer horizon since it's not bounded by physical mortality as a player's statistics are.

In both instances, it is our probability blindness that dims our understanding. That blindness leads us to impute meaning where none exists. We interpret random sequences as hot hands; stock losses are understood as harbingers of future gains; clusters of stars are seen as evidence of constellations.

Why we insist on finding our answers in stories instead of acknowledging the role of chance is not well understood. Gould has speculated that we may be seeking comfort, or struggling to keep confusion at bay. Some experts suggest that gains (like streaks, hot hands, or winning bets) are more memorable than losses, and therefore cloud our judgment. Because we (like Patrick) remember them more clearly than losses, we often believe they occur more often than they actually do.

Whatever the explanation, it's plain that we bring little inherent intuition into underlying frequencies when we are trying to make sense of what we observe. It does not seem to be in our DNA to "get" the concepts of distributions, or frequencies, or odds. Instead, we're drawn to the unique narratives, the individual stories. They sweep us away, especially if they end well. When they do, we ignore the role of luck and stress skill and intentions instead. Tales about iconic victors, heroic athletes, and specific achievements of all kinds win the day.

Our innate tendencies may explain why we allow a faith in the long-run safety of truly risky investments to dominate. The concrete story prevails. It is, after all, about gains to be garnered with supposed skill and then counted, savored, then consumed. Pitted against the more abstract and diffuse calculus of uncertainty, there is no contest.

In the Long Run We Are Dead

By now it should be clear that the long run is an impossible standard to apply.

If you are building a dynasty for the ages and have boundless resources, then stocks for the long run could be the best possible game plan. Losses should not faze you then—you'll never need to withdraw the money, and you'll have the resources to withstand all bear markets.

But for the rest of us, an extremely long-run standard does not suit our finite assets or mortal lives. To recall the aphorism attributed to John Maynard Keynes, "the market can stay irrational longer than you can stay solvent." As we've seen, target-date funds or other age-based strategies don't solve the problem because they may be locking in big losses at just the moment when they are switching from stocks to bonds.

Markets rise and markets fall, but it is folly to assume that they'll hit their best averages in perfect rhythm with your own explicit needs. Instead of placing your faith in the potential of an indefinitely long run, a more dependable choice is to focus on the needs of your one very particular run.

CHAPTER 6

Your Personal Risk Profile

All men should strive
To learn before they die
What they are running from, and to, and why.
                                        —James Thurber

So far, our discussion of risk has aimed to deepen your familiarity with the losing end of the risk–reward trade-off. The idea is not to warn you off all risk, but to illustrate why it's so important to choose risk wisely and well—so that losses, when they occur, are not ruinous. The best way to do this in an uncertain world is to determine your risk set point. This is the single most important investment decision you will make.

To guide you, you have your goals—and especially your needs, which dictate where your risk set point will lie. This approach works well because it is so specific. It defines your investment risk in a personal way—your risk is the chance of falling short of your goals, and not the volatility of what you own. The goal-driven approach also keeps risk manageable by separating your aspirational wants from your fundamental needs, which you cannot afford to place at risk.

In addition to your goals, you also have a distinct personal risk profile, which provides you with a second line of attack. Understanding this profile provides the chance to retest your risk set point. And it also serves the second purpose of helping you decide how audacious your risky zone can be.

But how can you bring your risk profile to light? A good approach is to amalgamate the objective view from outside and your subjective judgments from within. Both matter. Ideally, they will complement one another, although this does not always happen. There is considerable debate about whether people have inborn traits that predispose them toward taking or shunning risks, but you don't have to believe that risk preferences are predetermined in order to discern individual behavior patterns.

Read on to get a handle on both the objective and subjective sides of your risk profile. We'll also look in on Paul's group to see how they discover their personal risk portraits. As you begin exploring your own risk profile, you may get a more accurate result if you, too, work in a group or invite a partner to help. If you're not ready for a financial advisor, choose someone who is not too shy to give you an honest opinion.

Capacity for Audacity

To capture your risk profile, let's circle back again to the goals and the lifetime budget we developed in the first part of this book. The markers we've looked at—your goals and your potential lifetime earnings—are also key drivers of your objective risk capacity.

Goals: The Countdown

How close are you to meeting your goals? And how much time remains before you must begin to spend? Both elements affect how much risk you can take.

As an illustration, consider the difference between Julia and Sue in meeting their college education goals. Both are still far short of their goals, but Julia has 10 and 12 years to go. Sue, on the other hand, is already paying college tuition bills for her eldest—and expects to be doing so for the next few years. As you may recall from her time line in Chapter 2, she'll then get only a 3-year reprieve before her second boy graduates from high school.

Sue has much less time, so her yearly contributions will have to be larger than Julia's. And because she's still far short of her basic needs, she does not have the luxury of funding her aspirational goals. If Sue succeeds in getting her ex-husband to share the burden, as she thinks she may, then the two of them can revisit her plan.

Sue's bottom line, though, is that her college investments must stay almost entirely in the safety zone in order to fund her educational goals at their minimum level. Julia, on the other hand, has more time. The danger with long time horizons, of course, is that they can lull you into procrastination and inertia. Originally, as we've seen, Julia and Jim focused only sporadically on investing for college. Now that they've been stirred to attention, they see that they can contribute enough for each of the next 12 years to cover their minimum needs for two children and still have money left over. Those extra dollars for educational aspirations can go into risky investments.

As they monitor their progress, they may find it relatively easy to continue meeting their minimum saving requirements, with money to spare. If that happens, they can ratchet their minimalist scenarios several notches up and invest more money in their education safety zone. On the other hand, if Julia and her family are still comfortable with their minimalist scenarios, they can also adopt the reverse strategy and put additional money in their risky zone—just as long as their safety zone is on track to full funding.

In deciding whether to recalibrate risk, it's especially important to keep track of minimal needs. Having extra time to save makes an important difference. This is not because risks dissolve over the long haul, but for the simple reason that time adds more opportunities to save.

Your Future Earnings: The Flex Factor

Your human capital shapes not just your lifetime budget but also your objective capacity for risk.[1]

Lifetime income can be flexible or rigid. If it is not hard for you to increase the amount of money you can earn, your earnings are flexible. You may have an occupation that gives you opportunities to work extra hours—or extra years, as in the case of professions that let you delay retirement. Or your position may afford you the option of taking extra jobs. It should be straightforward to read your own "flex factor."

Because flexible income brings hidden growth potential to an individual's earnings power, it allows individuals to take more investment risk. They can partly meet their goals by working more, so flexible earners have greater ability to withstand losses. Their ability to add income through extra work is like a layer of insurance.

Both Julia and Sue have flexible income. Julia can add hours and projects, and Sue can increase her patient load. Both can delay their retirement if they choose. Sam and Patrick also have the flexibility of delaying their retirements, but they're not now in a position to add extra work. (For them, that would be moonlighting.)

People whose wages are more rigid lack these advantages. For them, lifetime earnings are relatively fixed and signal a reduced capacity for risk-taking. A manual laborer who can't work much beyond age 60 or 65—or a teacher approaching mandatory retirement—has less resilience to losses than, say, an attorney of the same age who is able to delay retirement for many years.

Age comes into play, too. People may take greater investment risks when young than old. This is not because their holding period is so long, though. Rather, the young have more time to reach their goals. Their future earnings horizon is long. And, because they typically have more opportunities to change their field of specialization while young, they often have more work flexibility as well.

Let's compare Patrick's income flexibility with Sam's. Although they share some characteristics, Patrick has far less flexibility because he is about 20 years older. You can easily imagine him protesting, ever ready to add opportunities to take risk. The rationale he likes is the one he's heard often from his broker: Even after he retires, he will need to own stocks for "growth"—because these days he can expect retirement to stretch 20 or even 30 years. According to conventional advice, this is long enough to ride out losses, but too long to outlast a safe portfolio with no "growth."

In retirement, though, Patrick will come close to exhausting his lifetime earnings power, with almost no potential earnings left. That's a powerful argument against taking a great deal of risk. The buffer he could get from his expected earnings is just about gone.

As a result, in retirement, it will make sense for him to monitor his set point frequently to make sure that he is still comfortable with it. He can test whether he still has faith in the minimum basic needs he's specified. If not, he can shift his set point and move more money into his safety zone.

In an interesting twist, though, the flex factor could actually expand Patrick's risk capacity after his official retirement. If, for example, he decides to start an encore career, with reasonable chances for success, he will change his risk capacity profile. As a human resources executive, he might consider hanging out a shingle as a consultant after retirement. He could try his hand at headhunting, for instance. Or he might find something entirely different. (Of course, he'll need some assurance of success before he can modify his risk settings.)

Without the added employment flexibility, though, Patrick would be ill-advised to think himself endowed with a large capacity for risk-taking in the market, especially after he retires.

Income Security and Risk

Work income can also be classified according to how risky or secure it is. You can gauge the riskiness of your earnings by such features as the terms of employment and the ease of finding a new position in the event of an unexpected termination. People in secure positions include tenured teachers and professors, doctors, nurses, civil servants, and plumbers. Insecure occupations include freelancing, contracting, architecture, and human resource management, among many others.

Another yardstick for judging the riskiness of earnings is the explicit connection a position bears with the general economy. Some sectors are more closely affected by the business cycle than others. Real estate, construction, and financial services are clear examples. Others, such as health care, are less touched by dips in market demand.

The riskier your occupation, the greater the impact of the market on your earnings will be, and the smaller your risk capacity. This is true regardless of your age. When your lifetime income potential is insecure, it's better to mitigate market exposure by putting less money, not more, in risky assets.

So, for example, investment bankers and stockbrokers—whose livelihood depends on the market—should manage their stock exposure with this vulnerability in mind. This guideline runs counter to the misleading conventional wisdom that urges people to "invest in what you know." But for financial professionals who own a lot of stocks, a downturn would hit doubly hard.

Family Ties

Another risk indicator lies in your family circle. Who depends on you? Do you have family members in poor health? Ailing parents who will need care? Relatives who may need your help in the future?

We are creatures of connection. We are bound closely with others—usually family members—who have strong claims on our emotional and financial support. You probably do not need to be told about these real or potential demands, but it's easy to overlook them when you sit down to rate your ability to take risk. Yet these claims on your pocketbook can put a squeeze on your risk capacity.

Another way to think about family claims is to list them as potential needs—alongside your actual ones. Then, it's a judgment call to evaluate their likelihood, magnitude, and potential urgency.

Claims can come from outside your family too, depending on your circumstances and choices. One couple we know, for instance, is childless, but has made it their long-term mission to help send the daughters of a widowed close friend to college. For them, this has meant cutting back a little on everyday spending in order to set aside enough for their extra goal. And, because they consider the endeavor essential and not optional, the threshold on the risk they can take here is moderate to low.

Measuring Risk Capacity

It's an art, not a science, to assemble all these elements into an overall measure of risk capacity. Julia, for example, was taken aback to discover that her risk capacity is moderate to high, even though she is an entrepreneur and can't always predict her income from year to year.

It took the group nearly an hour to persuade her that, by objective criteria, she has more capacity to take risk than she had believed, even without including her recent inheritance.

Julia's bonus has come from her flexibility—to work extra projects, earn more income, and delay retirement for many years. It's true that as a landscaper she has exposure to the real estate market that puts her earnings at risk. But she has learned how to insulate herself from the real estate doldrums. She has created an education niche that's less tied to the housing market—a teaching gig at the local community college, special education projects at a few local nurseries, and more.

In addition, her family income is stabilized considerably by her husband Jim's teaching salary. Jim's tenure means that his position is secure, if much less flexible than Julia's (although Jim does have flexibility reserves during the summer months). As a family, their future income from work allows them to take a fair amount of risk. In addition, at 42 and 44 years old, Julia and Jim are still reasonably young, with many years of work ahead of them.

When Julia puts her family's goals and needs into the picture, she's pleased to learn that they are comfortably able to set money aside to cover their basic future needs without crimping their current life style. These needs include college plans for two children and retirement.

Julia's parents are reasonably well heeled, with a modest pension in addition; and should things take a turn for the worse, she has two brothers who are willing and able to help out. So family is not a great worry. Jim's parents are both deceased.

You might expect Sue to rate a similar capacity for risk in light of her high income and her flexible, secure employment. This is the first view expressed by several group members. But this time it is Sue who pushes back. She realizes only too well that she is now a single parent—and her goals include sending three children to college. She can't count on her ex-husband for much help with their children's education. Not only is she is far from meeting her basic educational goals, but her fixed living expenses, including child care and housekeeping, are relatively high. Divorce has shrunk her risk capacity dramatically.

Her retirement accounts are low in comparison with her goals too. And she needs to keep the needs of her parents in mind. They are in good health, living modestly within their means, and well insured. Still, they are elderly, and Sue has just one sister who could help out in case their health should fail. Sue is almost 50, and she still has many years of work ahead of her—but not enough to tip the risk scales in the direction of high risk taking.

Sam's case is harder to pin down. At first, his friends are stumped. He is in many ways a blank slate. He's skilled in his profession, with a good resume. At 38, he has prospects of long, profitable employment. Sam's family claims are minimal, and he has no dependents. His parents live in Canada, where they are in good health and well insured. Based on this profile, you'd expect him to have a high capacity for risk taking.

But Sam has just suffered a long bout of unemployment. On the other hand, as a marketing professional, he has the ability to shift out of the technology sector and into a different industry. Sam's work flexibility is also nuanced. As long as he goes on working as a corporate employee he can't add hours or extra income. At the same time, he has the flexibility to delay his retirement for many years if he needs to.

Score him moderate to moderately high, on balance. To the extent that he can rely on his future income to meet his goals, he can afford to make risky investments. Sam has a hard time stipulating his goals and needs with any precision. He has no clear vision of what that next phase of his life will look like. Still, he says he wants to settle down some time soon, and he imagines that a house, a mate, and children will all be part of the picture.

He also has no clue about the lifestyle he wants during retirement. It's too far away. He knows the day will come for him to retire, but he knows he has not yet established the lifestyle that he'd want to sustain into his golden years. And retirement feels irrelevant to him in any case. The only exception to his blackout on retirement has been his 401(k). He's been a long-time participant, drawn in because the plans looked too good to pass up. He was motivated by the tax deferrals and the matching money that his former employers all contributed.

Sam spends a lot of time puzzling over how to pull all these observations together to rate his overall risk capacity. The verdict from the group, finally, is that his capacity is moderate to high, based on the long stream of income he can expect. Their judgment is also based on his age and his potential work flexibility.

Sam's circumstances are sure to evolve. He's smart to be starting his planning early, because his longer investing horizon will enable him to accumulate more. He plans to monitor his assessments and refine them as his plans come into focus over time.

Patrick feels he has learned a lot from this discussion—especially in understanding how his human capital affects his capacity to take risk. It's an angle he has not considered before.

He now understands that his diminishing reserves of income potential reduce his capacity for risk. Unsurprisingly, though, he takes the buoyant view that he will beat the rap by extending his work flexibility. He will either delay retirement or launch an encore career. He is confident he can overcome all obstacles and succeed. But he realizes he can't count on any of this quite yet.

He also recognizes that the sector he works in, human resources, is risky, because its fortunes are linked to the unemployment rate in the economy. Always the optimist, though, he considers his position safe, not risky. He runs a small department where people rely on his knowledge and seniority. He's actually been busier than ever during the downturn, wearing many hats in his firm and taking charge of hiring temporary contractors. His wife Marianne has a secure job, although it does not pay well and gives her little income flexibility.

Patrick and Marianne have few potential claims from their family. Their children are grown and independent. All four of their parents are deceased. On the other hand, Patrick is behind on his goals. He still has to stretch to meet his basic retirement needs but has perhaps a dozen years left to reach them.

Patrick's overall risk capacity is low. He should consider moving his set point and expanding his safety zone by saving more, or by shifting money from his risky investment zone. Other options include active planning for ways to save more—by boosting his income or cutting his current spending if possible. He can also consider delaying his retirement.

Risk Tolerance

Your *ability* to take risk is entirely different from how you *feel* about risk. Risk capacity is an objective measure that reflects how much money you can afford to lose, even in a worst case, without impairing your minimal goals. But how you feel about risk is subjective. It's not necessarily tethered to rational thought. Your risk *preference,* or tolerance, reflects how willingly you expose yourself to loss in exchange for the possibility of gain.

Sometimes referred to as the "sleep factor," risk tolerance runs the gamut between thrill-seeking behavior and dread. Time and again, Patrick takes risks willingly, but Sam does not. Of the two, ironically, it is Sam who has the greater objective capacity for risk.

These two measures are equally valid takes on your personal approach to risk. But they are not equally useful in directing your investment decisions.

It's your risk *capacity* that sets limits on how much risk you can take. Hand in hand with your goals, risk capacity dictates the size of your safe and risky zones. The constraints that it generates are firm.

Your feelings about risk, on the other hand, play a secondary role. This is important to emphasize, because so many popular financial web sites would have you think otherwise. Many of them use a brief attitude quiz to generate an elaborate investment plan, as though your risk tolerance can be gauged on the run and then magically mixed with your time horizon to bake up your ideal asset allocation.

Where risk preferences do count, though, is in your risky zone. They can help guide you to the level of risk that is comfortable, once you've set up a right-sized safety zone. If you are like Patrick, whose appetite outstrips his capability, knowing your risk preferences is a first step toward taming your animal spirits. On the other hand, if you are like Sam—who has become more timid than he needs to be—then recognizing your hesitance can help nudge you into a more rational stance. Understanding your attitude to financial risk can also help you spot (and avoid) common behavioral and cognitive mistakes.

Rating the Raters: Good Tests and Bad

The best questionnaires will be administered and discussed by good financial advisors. There is also a smattering of good testing material available at no charge on the Internet.[2]

Typical questions will inquire about your past and present investment behavior, weighing such attitudes as how regretful (or resilient) you are after you lose money. Another good question asks whether you focus on gains or possible losses when you invest. (Individuals who evenhandedly consider both possibilities appear to be rare.) There are also hypothetical investment scenarios inviting you to specify how much pain you are willing to risk in exchange for different levels of gain.

Questionnaires often ask you to rate yourself on how much risk tolerance you believe you have. Many people answer this question quite accurately, but not everyone gets it right. And tests occasionally weigh psychological traits like skepticism or impulsivity, which, though separate from your risk tolerance, may be related.

Caution is in order, though, as you review the offerings available to you under the rubric of risk tolerance. Most of the questionnaires circulating on the Web are of dubious quality and reliability.[3] Beware of five-point tests, which are ubiquitous but much too short. Most experts agree that a test must capture enough information to be reliable. That probably means no less than 20 or even 25 questions.

Other problems with risk questionnaires—as flagged by Geoff Davey, who owns and leads a prominent risk-profiling company in Australia—include a proclivity for irrelevant questions. Queries about circumstances— age, marital status, or number of dependents—do not relate to your tolerance for risk. Including them produces distortions.[4]

Yet another issue stems from the way the questions are presented. As we saw in Chapter 5, framing affects our behavior in subtle but critical ways. Add to this the fact that we live in a culture that admires risk taking, and you can understand why questionnaires can yield biased results. Many respondents, not wanting to appear wimpy, give answers that are not sincere.

Perhaps you've stumbled across a questionnaire that asks about your taste for physical risk—as in, "Do you enjoy jumping out of small airplanes?" This is a test you can toss. Even psychologists who back the proposition that risk tolerance is a stable personality trait have nevertheless concluded that physical and financial risk tolerance are completely different attributes. One does not translate to the other. Psychologists talk about four separate types of risk preferences—physical, social, ethical, and financial—with scant interrelationship among them.

The Value of Testing

Within the category of financial risk, many analysts have portrayed risk attitudes as stable traits etched deeply into personality. But critics counter that risk preference is a state rather than a trait and therefore quite changeable.

The controversy rolls on. But for us, the results of high-quality tests are useful tools either way. The key is to view them in the context of your goals and risk capacity—and not on their own.

When used this way, risk tolerance questionnaires can expose contradictions like Patrick's between risk capacity and risk preference. Paired with his capacity assessment, the risk tolerance questionnaire has delivered Patrick the jolt he needs.

The risk score Patrick received has also marked the start of a long conversation with Marianne, whose risk tolerance is, unsurprisingly, much lower. Instead of the usual recriminations and anger, their exchange this time has been a relatively calm and constructive search for accord. This they attribute to the test scores. They have not in truth received new information, but now it is framed by the test experience. And Patrick concedes that some taming of his risk appetite is in order.

Fortunately, there are good solutions available—even if he cannot curb his ample tolerance for risk.

To ensure that his safety zone stays big enough—and appropriately invested in safe, inflation-protected bonds—he can put some of his key investing decisions on autopilot. He can step out of the decision loop by preselecting his 401(k) options at work and can also enroll in an automatic contribution plan with his bank, investment manager, or trusted advisor.

Of course, Patrick can also work on spotting his irrational behavior and trying to mend his ways. He can try to learn to nip overconfidence in the bud, for instance. This is a worthy endeavor—but it won't be easy and it will take time. In the meantime, he can rely on the shortcuts of automating and getting outside help.

And there you have it—a short guide to discovering your own personal risk profile. Add this profile to your personal destinations, and you are well on your way toward creating a reliable investment plan tailored for you.

III
PART

BUILDING BLOCKS

CHAPTER 7

Finding the Safe Investment Zone

A nickel ain't worth a dime any more.

—Yogi Berra

Y ou may remember the earnest young couple in their swank online kitchen. Back in Chapter 4, Sam debunked their story for its naive advocacy of stocks. In their video, they claimed that conventional Treasury bonds or certificates of deposit can be risky because your dollars are apt to lose buying power—and on this score they were right. Treasurys and CDs, the trusty, sleep-at-night prescription, can be anything but safe in inflationary times.

Yet, not so long ago, these were the only options available to investors in search of safety. At first blush, they seem utterly secure: after all, the principal of U.S. Treasury bills, notes, and bonds is guaranteed by the full faith and credit of the United States, and the risk of default on interest payments has been slim to none.

Bank CDs also come with guarantees. These deposits, which are meant to stay put for a stated period of time, are guaranteed as long as they fall within specified dollar limits.

The guarantees are backed by insurance from the FDIC, a federal government agency.

But when inflation appears—as it has, regularly, in modern times—conventional Treasurys and CDs become not a haven but a treacherous rabbit hole.

A safe investment must allow you to buy the essentials that you've targeted. It's the asset that should produce the cash you need—to buy what you need, when you need it. When Treasurys don't keep pace with inflation, your money won't pay for the groceries, the rent, or the education you've planned when the bills come due.

Today there are better options. In 1997, the U.S. Treasury introduced inflation-linked bonds, which guarantee principal *and* protect investors against inflation.

If you were to consider only outdated alternatives, you might be blindsided, much as the earnest young couple in the promotional video was deceived. But inflation-linked Treasurys and savings bonds do provide the safety that conventional Treasurys lack. Stocks do not.

Inflation: The View from Your Destination

Why care so much about inflation?

Paul's gang all wondered why inflation should be such a preoccupation. All of them said that "mild inflation," at 2, 3, or 4 cents on the dollar, did not worry them—even though they understood that the money is irretrievably lost year after year.

Do you agree? To gauge your own attitude, try the quiz in Table 7.1.

If your answers cluster toward the right-hand side of the page, they reveal a weak inflation antenna. But you are not alone. When inflation hovers between 1.5 and 4 percent, as it has in the recent past, most of us shrug it off as tame and benign. Concern tends to grow only when inflation starts climbing at a higher rate.

It's surprisingly difficult to develop a realistic appreciation of inflation's effects—especially if you're shielded by

Table 7.1   "What Is Your Risk Attitude?" Quiz

Question	Often	Sometimes	Rarely/Never
Are you concerned about your investments' ability to stay abreast of inflation?	☐	☐	☐
When you're driving, do you pay close attention to prices as you pass gas stations? (If you don't drive, answer for supermarket prices.)	☐	☐	☐
When you think and plan for funding education (or other goals) in the future, do you adjust your investment targets to include the effects of inflation?	☐	☐	☐
When you think and plan for retirement, do you also think about how inflation will affect your spending power and your lifestyle later in life?	☐	☐	☐

wages or salary that keeps rising with the cost of living. But view inflation from the perspective of your goals, and the picture you get is suddenly sobering.

Take Patrick. In his late fifties, he now has enough information to estimate his retirement paycheck goal with reasonable accuracy. He's calculated that he will need $40,000 each year to supplement his social security checks and Marianne's. He has been paying little attention to inflation because he thinks it's been quite low.

Patrick expects to retire in 10 to 12 years. If there is no inflation at all, then Patrick should be able to cover the expenses he's expecting with a $40,000 paycheck, drawn annually from his investment account. In this happy scenario, Patrick meets his investment goals and gets to have everything he has planned for—all of it, the entire package.

If there is "mild" inflation, though, Patrick's supplemental $40,000 paycheck will cover only part of the package. Figure 7.1 shows just how much of his lifestyle he will be able to hang on to, and how much he will have to give up, if inflation runs at 3 percent—roughly the average level of the past 20 years. At this rate, mild inflation still cuts the lifestyle package back by over 25 percent in just 10 years.

Figure 7.1   Cumulative Effect of Inflation

If you extend the forecast out another 10 years, again assuming inflation of 3 percent per year, Patrick's current lifestyle gets cut to about 55 cents on today's dollar. That would reduce Patrick and Marianne's spending capacity by nearly half—just 10 years into retirement.

Your retirement goals are at particular risk from inflation—once you leave the workforce, you lose any inflation hedge you have enjoyed from wages or salary increases. Social Security payments do protect you with their cost-of-living adjustment, though it is the rare pension that keeps up with inflation.

Because your safety zone must fund your most basic needs, inflation protection is essential. Your lifestyle—and your goals—depend on it.

What's the Real Interest Rate Anyway?

This picture of vanishing spending power is a scary prospect. Patrick takes one quick look and acknowledges that he and Marianne will need to revise their target. Their investments will have to provide them with supplemental yearly income to buy what $40,000 will buy today.

In other words, the amounts they earn on their safe investments will need to keep up with inflation.

To help them accomplish this goal, Patrick and Marianne can use inflation-linked bonds. These come in two varieties: Treasury Inflation-Protected Securities, or TIPS, and U.S. government savings bonds with inflation protection, or I Bonds.[1]

As we've seen, the returns guaranteed on conventional Treasury instruments and CDs are not necessarily "for real" because they don't necessarily pace inflation. While you are holding them, there is always a possibility that inflation can jump above and beyond the stated interest rate you've been promised. At the end of the period, your money would then buy less for you than at the outset.

Nor can you be sure that inflation will be "mild" as it has in the recent past. In fact, inflation varies widely from decade to decade and from year to year, as you can see from Table 7.2. In the worst 10-year period, from 1973 to 1982, the cost of living more than doubled. As measured by the cost of a basket of commonly purchased goods and services, the price level was up 2.6 times. By contrast, in the decade between 1926 and 1935, prices *fell* at an average clip of 2.5 percent per year.

So, if inflation surprises you by spiking to 4 percent, but you've invested in a CD that earns only 2 percent, it is easy to see how you can fall behind. Your 2 percent return will be a return in name only—and that's exactly what it's called, a *nominal* return.

The risk of falling behind grows if your bond or CD has a long term. If inflation persists, the nominal returns that you sign up for will purchase less and less with each passing year. A medium- to long-term nominal bond, with a maturity of 5 to 30 years, exposes you to many years of inflation risk.

To see what your yearly return looks like when adjusted for inflation, simply subtract the annual inflation rate from the nominal rate. The result is a close approximation of your real return. In this example, because inflation is greater than the nominal return, your real return is negative.

But these are calculations that can be made only after the fact. No one can accurately predict future inflation. Nominal rates do contain some compensation for inflation—investors demand it—but this reflects expectations only. And expectations are often wrong.

This is the key to the apparent paradox of the risky risk-free rate. Both the future inflation rate and the future real

Table 7.2   U.S. Inflation Rates since 1926

Year	Percent Change in CPI-U	Year	Percent Change in CPI-U	Year	Percent Change in CPI-U	Year	Percent Change in CPI-U
1926	−1.1	1948	3.0	1970	5.6	1992	2.9
1927	−2.3	1949	−2.1	1971	3.3	1993	2.7
1928	−1.2	1950	5.9	1972	3.4	1994	2.7
1929	0.6	1951	6.0	1973	8.7	1995	2.5
1930	−6.4	1952	0.8	1974	12.3	1996	3.3
1931	−9.3	1953	0.7	1975	6.9	1997	1.7
1932	−10.3	1954	−0.7	1976	4.9	1998	1.6
1933	0.8	1955	0.4	1977	6.7	1999	2.7
1934	1.5	1956	3.0	1978	9.0	2000	3.4
1935	3.0	1957	2.9	1979	13.3	2001	1.6
1936	1.4	1958	1.8	1980	12.5	2002	2.4
1937	2.9	1959	1.7	1981	8.9	2003	1.9
1938	−2.8	1960	1.4	1982	3.8	2004	3.3
1939	0.0	1961	0.7	1983	3.8	2005	3.4
1940	0.7	1962	1.3	1984	3.9	2006	2.5
1941	9.9	1963	1.6	1985	3.8	2007	4.1
1942	9.0	1964	1.0	1986	1.1	2008	0.1
1943	3.0	1965	1.9	1987	4.4	2009	2.7
1944	2.3	1966	3.5	1988	4.4	2010	1.5
1945	2.2	1967	3.0	1989	4.6		
1946	18.1	1968	4.7	1990	6.1		
1947	8.8	1969	6.2	1991	3.1		

Data Source: U.S. Department of Labor, Bureau of Labor Statistics. ftp://ftp.bls.gov/pub/special
.requests/cpi/cpiai.txt

rate are unknown. Conventional Treasury rates are risk free only in the sense that they guarantee nominal principal. But their *real rate of return is uncertain until after the fact*. The guarantees don't protect investors against inflation surprises.

When you buy inflation-linked Treasury or savings bonds, though, your principal is guaranteed in real dollars. You are effectively preserving what your money can buy. And you are freed from the guesswork of predicting inflation.

It's worth emphasizing these seemingly simple points because there is so much misdirection about TIPS in popular financial commentary. As we write, in mid-2011, 5-year *real* interest rates stand at slightly negative levels. As a result, at least one well known financial journalist has wrongly advised that "holding TIPS will make you poorer," adding that anyone who invests in TIPS at a negative real yield is misguided. It's important to correct this erroneous view.[2]

There is a great deal of doubt about what inflation will be in the future. But there is nothing irrational about investing some of your wealth in TIPS at a negative interest rate in order to eliminate this uncertainty. It's the equivalent of giving up a small part of the principal, as an insurance premium, in exchange for a guarantee that the rest of the principal will hold its purchasing value no matter how high inflation turns out to be.

When you see a TIPS yield that's less than zero, this is precisely the trade-off that's on offer. The higher actual inflation turns out to be, the more valuable the hedge will be in hindsight—and vice versa.

To understand how unfounded the alarm bells about negative real rates have been, simply check out the alternative, the nominal Treasury bond with the same maturity, and compare.

If the real return on 5-year TIPS is *minus* half a percent, and the nominal return on conventional 5-year bonds is 1.0 percent, then it will take an actual inflation rate of 1.5 percent per year over the 5-year term to make them equivalent. That's what is meant when people say the "break-even" inflation rate is 1.5 percent. Even if actual inflation turns out to be lower, you won't earn less than the real return you signed up for, if you hold your bond until its maturity.

But if inflation winds up *higher* than the break-even 1.5 percent—say it even winds up *above* the 2.1 percent rate being forecast by the Philadelphia Federal Reserve in mid-2011— then TIPS will outperform conventional Treasurys. Holders of the nominal bond will be the ones who end up poorer.

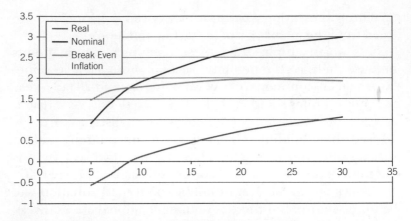

Figure 7.2   The Term Structure of Nominal and Real Interest Rates
Source: http://zvibodie.com/marketindicatorsview. This source is updated continually.

The point, though, is not to outperform conventional bonds. Rather, TIPS guarantee a *known* return in terms of consumer purchasing power—*regardless* of the actual rate of inflation, and even when real interest rates are negative. That makes TIPS the safest way to preserve the purchasing power of your wealth over time.

Remember that your safe investment zone is meant to ensure your future essentials, come thick or thin. It's not there to roll the dice on delivering your most aspirational goals.

If you find yourself rejecting safe investments because they are not profitable enough, you are asking the wrong questions. If you spurn insurance simply because the premiums put a crimp in your returns, you may be destined for disappointment—and possibly loss. As Sue might say, it's like looking for love in all the wrong places—and putting your prosperity at risk.

Real-Return Bonds

There is no better safe investment than inflation-linked government bonds. Let's look more closely at the two different kinds of real-return instruments that are available:

U.S. Treasury Inflation Protected Securities, known as TIPS, and inflation-protected U.S. government savings bonds, called I Bonds. Both are easy to understand. And, despite their big differences, each combines a fixed interest rate with an adjustable component that tracks inflation.[3]

I Bonds: Savings Bonds to Hedge Inflation

I Bonds are simple investments that are often overlooked. Like a savings account at a bank, I Bonds earn interest every month, and the accumulated amount of principal plus interest can never go down in value. The interest they earn will always be at least equal to the inflation rate, and if there is deflation, their value does not go down. Thus their nominal dollar value ratchets up with inflation, but does not go down with deflation.

Here is a list of their other key features. These instruments:

- Provide security because they are U.S. Treasury securities backed by the full faith and credit of the U.S. government
- Sell at face value, as a type of savings bond
- Do not trade in the market
- Offer liquidity and can be cashed in any time after 12 months
- Can never have a redemption value less than the amount that you paid for them
- Continue to earn inflation-indexed interest for up to 30 years
- Allow investments as small as $25 and as great as $5,000 per Social Security number each year, as explained below
- Have a tax advantage

A Composite Interest Rate   The interest rate on I Bonds has two components: one fixed and the other variable. Each May and November, the U.S. Treasury announces the fixed rate of return for all I Bonds issued in the next 6 months. This fixed rate remains in effect, unchanged, for the entire life of each bond—up to 30 years. The fixed rate will never be less than zero.

The second piece is variable, and it is added to the fixed rate. The variable component tracks inflation. Together, the fixed and variable components sum to the total composite interest rate on I Bonds.*

This means that I Bonds are guaranteed at least to meet inflation. If the fixed core rate is a positive number, then your bonds are guaranteed to beat inflation by the promised fixed rate.

The Inflation Adjustment Inflation is gauged via the U.S. Department of Labor's Consumer Price Index for All Urban Consumers (CPI-U), which is used for TIPS calculations as well. This index measures changes in prices paid by consumers for a specified basket of goods and services.

The inflation adjustment is announced each May and November as well—but, as mentioned, the variable (or adjustable) rate remains in effect only until the next semiannual announcement.

There is only a brief lag between the announcement and the time period that's measured. The May inflation component measures the change in the CPI-U from the end of the previous September through March; similarly, the inflation rate announced each November reflects the change in the index from March 31 through September.

Tax Advantage Like their nominal-rate conventional counterparts (EE savings bonds), I Bonds are not taxed until you redeem them—although you can elect to pay taxes currently. (Your election will hold as long as you own the bond.)

_____

*The sum is approximate because the total composite rate also includes one more very small term.

The interest that accrues and compounds semiannually is not actually paid out to you until you redeem your bond.

I Bonds thus have the advantage of tax deferral for as long as 30 years—and are not held inside a tax-deferred account. This tax advantage remains available no matter how much tax-deferred investing you do, and regardless of your income level.

Deflation Shield   If there is deflation, and consumer prices fall instead of rising, real interest rates turn negative. Deflation in any single 6-month period of the I Bond's life will automatically make the variable interest rate component negative. If there is deflation, the bond will therefore increase in value slowly or not at all.

The good news is that the *composite* interest rate on an I Bond can't go negative. If the consumer price level in any March/September span falls, the variable, inflation-tracking rate will be negative and will reduce the fixed-rate interest component. But the composite rate can never drop below zero.

At the very least, you can redeem I Bonds for what you paid, even if there is deflation continuously for 30 years (see Table 7.3). As you can see in Table 7.3, there has been only one 6-month period when the composite rate was zero— May to November 2009.

Where and How Much to Buy?   I Bonds are designed for small investors. Each Social Security number is limited to a total of $5,000 per year. Paper bond purchases are going away as of January 2012, so you must purchase I Bonds electronically from the Treasury. Electronic accounts are easy to establish at the Treasury Direct web site (treasurydirect.gov).

Despite these limits, it would be a mistake to dismiss I Bonds out of hand. The maximum purchase per couple can total up to $10,000 each year. (Until the elimination of paper bonds, the annual limit included an additional $5,000 per Social Security number in paper bonds.) Because of their

Table 7.3   I Bond Interest Rates since Their Introduction in 1998

Announcement Date	Annual Fixed Rate	Semiannual Variable Rate	Annualized Composite Rate at Announcement
Sept. 1, 1998	3.40%	0.62%	4.66%
Nov. 1, 1998	3.30%	0.86%	5.05%
May 1, 1999	3.30%	0.86%	5.05%
Nov. 1, 1999	3.40%	1.76%	6.98%
May 1, 2000	3.60%	1.91%	7.49%
Nov. 1, 2000	3.40%	1.52%	6.49%
May 1, 2001	3.00%	1.44%	5.92%
Nov. 1, 2001	2.00%	1.19%	4.40%
May 1, 2002	2.00%	0.28%	2.57%
Nov. 1, 2002	1.60%	1.23%	4.08%
May 1, 2003	1.10%	1.77%	4.66%
Nov. 1, 2003	1.10%	0.54%	2.19%
May 1, 2004	1.00%	1.19%	3.39%
Nov. 1, 2004	1.00%	1.33%	3.67%
May 1, 2005	1.20%	1.79%	4.80%
Nov. 1, 2005	1.00%	2.85%	6.73%
May 1, 2006	1.40%	0.50%	2.41%
Nov. 1, 2006	1.40%	1.55%	4.52%
May 1, 2007	1.30%	1.21%	3.74%
Nov. 1, 2007	1.20%	1.53%	4.28%
May 1, 2008	0.00%	2.42%	4.84%
Nov. 1, 2008	0.70%	2.46%	5.64%
May 1, 2009	0.10%	−2.78%	0.00%
Nov. 1, 2009	0.30%	1.53%	3.36%
May 1, 2010	0.20%	0.77%	1.74%
Nov. 1, 2010	0.00%	0.37%	0.74%
May 1, 2011	0.00%	2.30%	4.60%

Source: U.S. Treasury at http://www.treasurydirect.gov/indiv/research/indepth/ibonds/res_ibonds_iratesandterms.htm

security and their liquidity, I Bonds can fill in important gaps in your safety zone, even if they can't be your mainstay.

An excellent use for I Bonds is for emergency savings. Instead of parking your rainy-day money in a money market account, use I Bonds instead. That way, you'll be sure to keep pace with inflation. Just be careful to build a bridge for the first year, because I Bonds cannot be redeemed for 12 months after purchase. Create a short-term backup by banking some initial cash in parallel with your I Bonds. I Bonds redeemed before 5 years are subject to a small forfeiture of 3 months' interest—but chances are they will give you a better overall result in real terms than cash.

Treasury Inflation-Protected Securities (TIPS)

I Bonds are savings bonds, not marketable securities. They behave more like bank certificates of deposit than bonds. TIPS, on the other hand, work like bonds—they are traded in the marketplace. All Treasury bonds are simply loans made by bondholders to the U.S. Treasury for a stated term of 5, 10, or 30 years. In return for making the loan, the bondholder receives a regular, periodic interest payment, or coupon, every 6 months. At maturity, the Treasury agrees to repay the principal in full. *In the meantime, though, investors who wish to redeem their bonds must sell them in the market, and the price they will receive will depend on market conditions.*

Adjusting for Inflation Like conventional, nominal Treasury bonds, TIPS are issued at auction by the U.S. Treasury, with a fixed coupon interest rate and a stated maturity. Unlike nominal bonds, though, TIPS have an adjustment mechanism that allows them to keep up with inflation.

In contrast to I Bonds, it is the *principal* of TIPS that is adjusted to track inflation. The coupon rate stays the same.

Each month, an inflation adjustment is made to the principal of TIPS, based on the same index that is used for I Bond adjustments: the Consumer Price Index for Urban

Consumers (CPI-U). The adjustment uses a value with a 2-month lag, and is not seasonally adjusted.

This adjustment assures owners of TIPS that their principal will maintain its real value at maturity. Unlike owners of nominal bonds, TIPS investors do not face erosion of their principal by inflation over the life of their bond.

Although the coupon *rate* does not vary, the coupon *amount* automatically changes when the principal is adjusted for inflation. In this way, the investor ends up receiving a *fixed real return.*

Table 7.4 illustrates how the inflation adjustment works for a hypothetical $1,000 bond with a real coupon rate of 1.5 percent.

The original $1,000 face amount is called the bond's par value. It's the *real* dollar amount that the issuer will repay to the investor at maturity.

Table 7.4 presents adjustments and payments on an annual basis—but in practice, principal values get adjusted every month, while coupon payments are made every 6 months. The inflation factor tracks cumulative inflation from the bond's issuance date.

Deflation Floor   As Table 7.4 illustrates, increases in the bond's principal neutralize inflation. If there is consistent deflation, though, the adjustment factor gets smaller instead of larger, and the principal value will decline instead of growing—as it does in the hypothetical year 4 above. At maturity, investors

Table 7.4   TIPS Illustration

Period	Real Coupon Rate	Actual Inflation	Inflation Factor	Starting Principal	Adjusted Principal	Coupon Payment
Year 1	1.5%	0.0%	1.0000	$1,000.00	$1,000.00	$15.00
Year 2	1.5%	2.5%	1.0250	$1,000.00	$1,025.00	$15.38
Year 3	1.5%	3.0%	1.0580	$1,025.00	$1,055.75	$15.84
Year 4	1.5%	−1.0%	1.0474	$1,055.75	$1,047.42	$15.71
Year 5	1.5%	4.0%	1.0893	$1,047.42	$1,089.34	$16.34

receive either the original face amount, or the adjusted principal value—whichever is greater.

If you are worried about falling prices, be aware that deflation would have to be severe or persistent in order for the principal value of TIPS at maturity to fall back to its face-amount floor. In this example, you can see that the inflation factor at the end of 5 years is still greater than 1.0, despite a year of deflation in year 4.

Figure 7.3 shows an example of how the principal and interest increased for a TIPS issued in 1999 through its term.

Why Tax-Deferred Accounts Are the Right Way to Go Unlike I Bonds, TIPS are taxed by the IRS like conventional taxable bonds—on a yearly basis, and at the ordinary income rate. Taxes on TIPS also have an extra wrinkle—not only is their interest taxed, but the amounts that have been added to

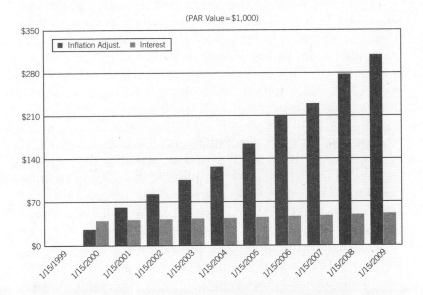

Figure 7.3   Cumulative Inflation and Annual Interest on the 3-7/8 Percent Treasury 10-year TIPS Due 1/15/2009

Source: http://www.treasurydirect.gov/indiv/research/indepth/tips/res_tips_rates.htm

principal as part of the inflation adjustment are also subject
to federal tax each year—at the ordinary income tax rate.
This tax is payable each year, even though the money is only
accrued and not distributed.

This tax treatment has two unwanted results. For one,
you owe tax each year on money that you do not receive.
(Some people call this a tax on "phantom income.") So you
must find the cash to pay elsewhere. In addition, federal
taxes will prevent you from achieving a tight hedge against
inflation. For this reason, TIPS are more efficiently held
in tax-deferred retirement accounts such as a 401(k), IRA,
Roth, or a deferred annuity. There, you avoid the phantom
income problem, and you achieve a far better hedge against
inflation. In a tax-deferred retirement account, you postpone taxes until you withdraw your money. In the case of a
Roth account, taxes may be permanently avoided.

Although it's important to recognize the tax drawbacks
of TIPS, these shouldn't be overstated. Nominal bonds are
also taxed in a similar fashion. Of course, nominal bonds
don't get adjusted for inflation—but expected inflation is
embedded in them, as we've seen. And, under the revenue
code we have, this expected inflation gets taxed too. It's
only in the tax on "phantom income" that TIPS taxes differ.
But you avoid this problem with tax-deferred accounts.

When Your Employer's Plan Does Not Offer TIPS   Like many people,
Patrick doesn't have a TIPS option available through his
employer's tax-deferred 401(k) plan. If you are in the same
situation, take some time to review all your tax-deferred
accounts. It would be a good idea to consult with a tax adviser
as you proceed.

If you have switched jobs, and have contributed in the
past to a 401(k) or to the non-profit 403(b) version, then you
most likely took the opportunity to move your money into a
self-directed rollover IRA. If so, this could be a suitable location for TIPS. If you've switched jobs but left your 401(k)
balances in your old employer's plan, consider rolling your

account over into an IRA and using it for TIPS investments. If you've established other self-directed IRAs, including Roth accounts, these may also be good places for TIPS. In the future, if you are eligible for a Roth account, make it a priority to contribute to one, because the tax treatment of Roth investments is extremely favorable, even though contributions are not deductible.

Finally, let your employer know you're not satisfied with the menu of choices they have given you, and tell them you want a TIPS option. Patrick is a key player in his company's human resources department, so he can readily talk to his peers in the next offices who are responsible for benefits decisions. Find the right person to speak with at your employer—and be persistent.

As we discuss below, there are a number of TIPS funds available today, most of which could be suitable for defined-contribution retirement plans. In addition, employers are increasingly adding a so-called "self-directed" option to their retirement plan line-ups. Self-directed accounts are a lot like brokerage accounts. The commissions charged for buying individual stocks or bonds make these accounts an expensive platform for continuous retirement contributions. But for individual TIPS and TIPS funds, they can be an efficient location.

The best way to buy individual TIPS in your tax-deferred account is at auction, using the commission-free online services of brokers who offer this feature.

Buying Guide for Individual TIPS

Purchasing individual TIPS is not difficult. Here is the lowdown on the most common ways to buy them.

At Auction with Treasury Direct. The Treasury issues TIPS four times each year—in January, April, July, and October, in maturities of 5, 10, and 30 years. Some of these are reopenings of recent auctions. It is possible to purchase TIPS directly from the U.S. Treasury by submitting

(Continued)

what's called a "noncompetitive bid." This assures you of receiving the full extent of your order. Just as in all Treasury auctions, you'll receive the same yield as successful competitive bidders. All you need to do is to set up an online account at Treasury Direct and link it with a bank account.

Unfortunately, Treasury Direct can be used for taxable accounts only. If it's your intention to place your TIPS in a taxable account, despite the tax inefficiency we've described, then this channel is for you.

At Auction with a Broker. You can buy TIPS for any tax-deferred accounts you maintain with a broker. If you make your purchases online, a few brokers—including Schwab and Fidelity—do not charge fees. At this writing, Vanguard will waive fees for online purchases of TIPS for clients with accounts larger than $100,000. This is a cost effective, tax deferred, and convenient way to purchase individual TIPS. Again, you are making what's called a noncompetitive bid. Noncompetitive bids are limited to $5 million per auction. A noncompetitive bidder by definition accepts the rate or yield determined at auction.

Secondary Market. TIPS are also available on the secondary market, but *we do not recommend that you go there* unless you have a great deal of experience. It won't be possible, otherwise, to gauge how reasonable a deal you are being offered. The retail markup is buried in the quote you'll receive, and if you're not experienced, you're likely to do much worse than the wholesale pricing you'd get at auction. (Even experience may not help you.)

Deflation Protection Is Better at Auction. In addition to advantageous pricing, a second benefit of buying at auction is that the bonds will be newly minted—or nearly so, if they are reopenings of auctions of recently issued, existing TIPS. Such bonds will not have much accumulated inflation. They'll therefore have low inflation factors—as illustrated in Table 7.3. Recall that TIPS have their principal adjusted for inflation every month, and that cumulative inflation is tracked by the inflation factor.

A low inflation factor provides deflation protection. Because the bond's face amount at maturity is guaranteed, you have a good deflation shield as long as you purchase the bond for close to its face amount and not much more.

Buying individual TIPS at auction limits you to the Treasury's rather minimal offering schedule, and it also confines you to maturities of 5, 10 and 30 years. It's possible to build a TIPS ladder even with these basic materials, as we'll see, but you can also buy TIPS with a blend of maturities through a fund.

Table 7.5   Real-Return Bonds at a Glance[4]

	I Bonds	TIPS
Inflation Adjustment	Twice-yearly adjustments in the interest rate that correspond with changes in the Urban Consumer Price Index (CPI-U).	Daily—by modifying the principal value to correspond with changes in CPI-U. Cumulative inflation since issuance is tracked via an inflation factor.
Interest	Interest payments have two components—a fixed-rate piece, which remains unchanged through the life of each bond, and a variable component, which reflects the most recent change in the CPI-U. Every 6 months, a new fixed rate is announced for new bonds issued in the 6-month period following the announcement date.	Fixed. Because the principal of TIPS is continually adjusted to reflect inflation, the *amount* of the coupon payment keeps changing. This results in a fixed real rate of return.
Maturity	Up to 30 years.	5, 10 and 30 years.
Purchase Limits	Each Social Security number is entitled to a maximum of $5,000 a year in electronic bonds.	No purchase limit.
Fees	No fees.	No fee for purchases from TreasuryDirect (although these are taxable accounts). Some brokerage firms charge no fees for online purchases.
Price Fluctuation	Prices do not fluctuate, although interest accrues. Can be redeemed after 12 months at their accrued value. Redemption value is never lower than the original purchase price.	Prices fluctuate with changes in real interest rates. If held directly and to maturity, price fluctuation should not be relevant.
Tax Treatment	Interest is accrued and not taxed until the I Bond is redeemed.	Interest is taxed on a current basis. Adjustments to principal are also taxed, even though these are not distributed until maturity. Best held in a tax-deferred account.

Buying TIPS Funds   In addition to purchasing individual TIPS, you can also buy TIPS funds—which include both mutual funds and TIPS exchange-traded funds, or ETFs. TIPS funds are convenient and have many advantages. But they have features that cause them to behave differently from individual TIPS in certain circumstances, so it's a good idea not to treat TIPS funds as perfect substitutes for individual TIPS.

Both funds and ETFs provide a low-cost way of buying a portfolio of TIPS of varied maturities. With funds, you no longer have to wait for an infrequent auction date to invest, and many funds allow you to invest relatively small amounts.

An ETF behaves more like a stock than a fund, even though it is made up of a portfolio of securities. With some important exceptions, a commission is charged upon ETF purchase and sale. As a result, if ETF commissions are not waived, it's better to choose a mutual fund rather than an ETF if you plan to make multiple purchases.

Most of these funds, but not all, are passively managed—they seek to buy diversified maturities without trying to search out mispriced securities for potential appreciation. As a result, most have low operating expense ratios. In addition to broad-based TIPS mutual funds, there are also funds that concentrate on shorter, intermediate, or long maturities.

Another advantage of TIPS funds and ETFs is that you can automate the reinvestment of your coupons—a pesky task that presents a housekeeping challenge to investors in individual TIPS. And, if for some reason you choose to place the funds in a taxable account, fund record-keeping simplifies your tax reporting. In addition, ETFs and mutual funds are required by law to distribute any inflation-generated increases in principal, so the phantom income problem does not arise in taxable accounts. These funds are still not tax efficient, but the problem of paying tax on income you don't receive is eliminated.

As good as they may be, TIPS funds are not necessarily your preferred option. One of the best ways you can minimize risk with TIPS is by building them into a ladder to match your upcoming needs once you stop working.

We'll have much more to say about laddering and matching in the next chapter. The idea is to start creating a paycheck for life, postdated to arrive during retirement. Laddering requires you to buy individual TIPS with different maturities and hold them until they come due. Matching maturities, and amounts, with your future spending timetable is a reliable way to reduce uncertainty.

On the other hand, owning a TIPS fund instead of holding individual TIPS to maturity exposes you to the risk that real interest rates may rise. When this happens, the value of the bonds owned by the fund will fall. And, because all fluctuations in real interest rates will affect your fund's value, TIPS funds are likely to provide you with an imperfect hedge against inflation. Longer-dated bonds are more susceptible to this risk than shorter ones.

As risks go, this one is relatively small. The value of a nominal bond fund, which does not keep investors abreast of inflation, will fluctuate more. Real interest rates are less volatile than nominal rates.

And there are many times when a TIPS fund may nevertheless be the best choice. Sometimes, buying individual TIPS for laddering is impractical, and some investors are not ready to begin laddering with TIPS.

Sam, for example, has a Vanguard TIPS fund available to him through his new employer's 401(k) plan. By choosing this fund, Sam will get the tax-deferred status that's so important for TIPS investments. His other tax-deferred options are limited in comparison, so the Vanguard fund in his 401(k) plan is an attractive choice.

Another reason that he is a good candidate for the fund is his age. As he has told the group, he has a hard time even imagining retirement—not to mention establishing firm spending goals for his golden years. He is unsure of what his eventual standard of living will be. TIPS funds give him a

Buying Guide for TIPS Funds

Just as you have different options for buying individual TIPS, you'll also face a number of choices when deciding how to invest in a TIPS fund. Here are a few guidelines.

Passive Management. TIPS Index funds that are passively managed tend to provide a better hedge than actively managed funds, which are aiming not for a hedge but for return.

Costs. Expenses add up over time, so it's a good idea to find the lowest-cost providers. The good news is that passively managed funds tend to have low operating expense ratios. But don't take this on faith. Verify.

Duration. Different funds often have different durations. Try to match duration to your own personal investing horizon to the extent possible.

Tax Location. As with individual TIPS, try to own your TIPS funds in a tax-deferred account if possible. TIPS funds are taxed in the same way as individual TIPS.

Distributions. Instruct the fund company to reinvest your distributions. If you own an ETF, have the brokerage reinvest automatically. It's often possible to avoid costs associated with reinvesting.

bridge opportunity to invest safely until he's ready to think more concretely about retirement.

There are quite a few TIPS mutual funds available. Vanguard's Inflation-Protected Securities Fund has among the lowest mutual fund expense ratios around. TIPS ETFs are not as plentiful, but their expense ratios tend, on the whole, to be lower. If you own them for a long time, any initial commissions may be offset by the lower expense ratios.

Different TIPS ETFs are available from iShares (TIP) and SPDR (TIPS). PIMCO offers a new twist, perhaps emblematic of changes to come. A few of its passively managed TIPS funds have different durations: There is one broad U.S. Index Fund, a 1–5 Year TIPS Index Fund, and a 15+ Year U.S. TIPS Index Fund. Speaking generally, it is fair to say that longer-term TIPS offer more effective inflation protection than TIPS that are held for only a short time. On the other hand, the 1–5 Year TIPS Index Fund has less exposure to real interest-rate risk because its portfolio has so short an average term.

Putting It All Together

This completes our survey of real-return government bonds.[5] In reviewing their key features, we've seen why they are unsurpassed in providing a default-free route to inflation protection. Both TIPS and I Bonds thus have an important role to play in securing the baseline outcomes you can't take chances on.

What's the best way to make these bonds work for you? How should you assemble TIPS and I Bonds in your safe investment zone? These questions take us back full circle to your underlying goals and how you break them down into wants and needs.

In the next two chapters, we'll shift our focus from the instruments to the orchestra. We'll zero in on two very common goals—education and retirement. And we'll look at ways to deploy real-return bonds, along with other appropriate low-risk investments, to help you reach your target destinations.

CHAPTER

8

The Art of Matchmaking

As for the future, your task is not to foresee it, but to enable it.

—Antoine de Saint-Exupéry

Choosing inflation-linked bonds is a good first step to safer investing. But what's the right mix for you? The reflexive answer, simply assembling TIPS or I Bonds helter-skelter, is more common than you might imagine. There are better approaches—including one we'll call "matchmaking."

Even in the realm of safer instruments, you can improve the odds of reaching your goals if you choose investments to match. This means choosing the right amounts and also considering the maturity dates of your investments.

In this chapter, we'll look more closely at the technique of matching your investments with the spending outcomes you desire or need, and we'll survey some other ways to assemble safer, goal-directed portfolios.

We'll start with retirement, a goal everyone needs to think about.

Creating a Ladder for Retirement

A simple technique for hedging your spending needs in retirement is to create TIPS "ladders."

If you line up the maturity dates of your TIPS with your spending deadlines, you'll have an extremely close fit with your needs, no matter what inflation—or interest rates—have been in the meantime. This is good matchmaking.

You'll recall that TIPS values fall when real interest rates rise and vice versa. Although real rates are less volatile than nominal ones, both do fluctuate. But, as we have seen, these fluctuations are not relevant when you hold individual TIPS until they mature. No matter how much the real rate has fluctuated during the term, you receive the same amount at maturity—the principal value, adjusted for inflation (but never less than par value if there has been cumulative deflation).

A TIPS ladder gives you the do-it-yourself equivalent of an inflation-protected partial annuity. The best way to buy your individual TIPS is at auction, in a tax-deferred account, at a brokerage that charges you no fees to buy them.

Because you're aiming to match your ladder as closely as you can to your spending dates, your choice of maturities will be dictated by your spending timetable. But TIPS ladders take forethought, because TIPS come in only three maturity terms—5, 10, and 30 years—and they are auctioned only four times each year. To take advantage of the 30-year maturities, it's good to start early.

Let's look at an example. Julia wants to start building her retirement TIPS ladder now. Following Paul's advice, she's aiming to match her investments with her spending: She does not expect Social Security to cover the needs that she and Jim foresee in retirement. To do a good job, they'll need to coordinate their buying in their tax-deferred accounts that they've normally done separately.

Jim's options are more limited than Julia's, but he has an IRA rollover account he can tap from an early 10-year stint he once did at another employer. Although Julia and Jim are far from sure about their target retirement date, they feel they can conservatively plan to retire when they are 67 and 69. Because they're extending their planning horizon to ages 87 and 89, they have 20 years to cover. Their total horizon starts in 25 years and ends 45 years from today.

Julia gulps at the audacity of a 45-year planning period. She's happy to have her group there with her to share the amazement, which is probably tinged with a little fear. Behind the awe they are all experiencing is the realization that they might not ever plan their investments so deliberately if left on their own.

Paul suggests that Julia and Jim ought to consider extending their plans even further, given today's growing life expectancies, but Julia resists.

Because Julia and Jim are starting to build their ladder now, they have 15 years to keep buying the longest-dated TIPS before they hit the 45 year mark. But the first five years of their planned retirement are less than 30 years away, so they will have to purchase 10-year TIPS and then "renew" them by rolling them when they come due into new 10-year TIPS. Because TIPS maturity terms are limited to 5, 10, and 30 years, they will have to take some rollover risk.

As a practical matter, you may encounter similar limitations. After all, we've been discouraging you from buying TIPS on the secondary market—you'll have a hard time evaluating the prices you are offered there. In addition, there are currently about 10 years with no TIPS maturing at all, even on the secondary market. The Treasury recently discontinued 20-year TIPS and resumed issuing them in 30-year maturities—causing these gaps to appear.

I Bonds can help fill the void. Each Social Security number is entitled to $5,000 in I Bonds each year so Julia and Jim could invest up to $10,000 more per year in I Bonds to fill gaps in their ladder. I Bonds have more flexibility than TIPS, because their prices do not fluctuate. I Bonds can be redeemed any time after the first year. Because I Bonds have tax advantages, they don't need to be purchased from a tax-deferred account either. Along with the added flexibility, though, I Bonds generally (but not always) provide a lower return than TIPS.

As an alternative, PIMCO currently has mutual funds for sale that are similarly based on portfolios of laddered TIPS.[1] These are geared to make monthly distributions of real income until each fund's final maturity date. There are no other funds backed by TIPS ladders yet, but these are something to watch for.

Why Match Dates?

You may have heard bond laddering advice before. Often, the rationale for laddering is diversification into multiple maturities. That's because interest rates vary according to the term or holding period. On any given date, the interest rates for 5-year bonds are highly likely to differ from rates on 30-year bonds. Generally—but not always—longer maturities carry higher interest rates.

The motivation behind the TIPS ladder, though, is *not* diversification but hedging.

Matched ladders pair investments with spending dates. They resort to "rolling" only as required by practical limitations. By matching maturities to spending needs in retirement, you hedge the risk of coming up short.

Diversification is entirely different. It's the principle of not putting all your eggs in one basket. It's a sensible way to try to cushion disaster—but it's no guarantee.

By contrast, a successful hedge is close to a sure bet. And, when it comes to your essentials, a good hedge is what you're after. TIPS, for example, can provide a default-free hedge against inflation risk, and they keep you out of the stock market's ups and downs. When they are laddered to match your future spending needs, they provide some protection against changes in real interest rates too.

Another—unexpected—advantage of laddering is the discipline it imposes. When you create a blueprint for your matched TIPS ladder, it concentrates your mind wonderfully on your life in the distant future—an exercise that's hard to manage otherwise.

Goals, after all, are dreams with deadlines. You can't make them real unless you start holding them to schedule. At the same time, if you—like Sam—are not ready to imagine your ladder, choose a TIPS fund with an average maturity close to the time when you expect more certainty.

Do You Need a "Reset" Moment?

As you get older, you gain more certainty about your needs during retirement. You're clearer on the lifestyle you want to maintain. You have an increasingly accurate idea of how much income this will require. And you're starting to think more specifically about when your retirement might begin.

In addition, your estimates of supplemental income from any defined benefit pension, or from Social Security—which many Americans have begun to worry about—are closer to the mark than ever before. The same is true for estimated Medicare benefits as compared to health care costs.

On the other hand, we've seen how investment risks are magnified once you retire. Without the buffer of inflation-adjusted earnings, inflation has a sharper edge. And market volatility hurts all the more once you start withdrawing money, especially if losses come early. As a result, the protections of your safety zone become especially important in retirement.

As you approach retirement, then, it makes a lot of sense to reassess your risk set point. Your foresight is better and your risks are about to shift into higher gear. Five to 10 years before you expect to retire, start with a serious review of both the income you'll require as well as the timing of your retirement.

(In case you've lost track of your original estimates, we'll walk you through the key steps of income reassessment in the discussion of annuities below.)

Use this new information to retest your risk set point. Is the minimum income produced by your safe investment zone really enough? Or is it time to shift more assets into safety? Because market volatility is such a serious threat in the withdrawal phase of life, be wary of a reverse reset toward more risk.

Try this thought experiment too: Figure out how much lifetime retirement income you would get if you moved *all* your investments into your safety zone. You can use a combination of laddered TIPS and life annuities, as described below, to guide your calculations. You may find that you can lock in more income via safe investments than you'd thought possible. Either way, use what you learn to help you expand your safety zone allocation.

If this exercise catches you up short, though, there is another, different reset option you can consider—postponing your retirement, or phasing it in more gradually than you once planned, or launching a new "Third Age" career. You can also try to find ways to save more.

Repeat this exercise periodically. About a year before you expect to retire is an especially good time to reflect yet again on your risk set point. You may find yourself weighting the inflation and market risks of retirement more heavily right around this time. It would be wise to allay your new concerns by shifting some investments away from risk.

The Power of Annuities

As effective as your TIPS ladder can be in protecting you from inflation and market volatility, there is one risk that a homemade TIPS annuity can't hedge. That's the real danger of outliving your money.

Actuarial studies show that nearly 1 in 3 women who are turning 65 years old now will live to be 90. Nearly one 65-year-old man in 5 will reach age 90. And the overall odds of living *beyond* 90 are as high as 1 in 4 when you consider only healthy people.

Even if they stick diligently with their audacious planning through age 88, Julia and Jim could be out of luck.

The closest way to hedge this most dreaded outcome is with a life annuity. A life income annuity also guarantees you a predictable "paycheck" in retirement. Inflation protection is also available—and advisable. With a steady monthly paycheck, you are freed from worrying about the ups and downs of your investment balance.

Because Julia is not ready to start thinking about life in 50 years, an annuity is a good solution for her. She and Jim can postpone this step, as she prefers to do, until the two of them approach actual retirement many years from now. To accommodate an annuity strategy, Julia and Jim can rethink their TIPS ladder. Instead of extending their ladder well into their seventies and eighties, they can plan to allocate more money to TIPS that mature earlier in their retirement. This will give them more flexibility to purchase annuities with their maturing TIPS at that time.

They can then consider a single premium immediate annuity (SPIA), which is exactly what its name suggests. In exchange for a onetime initial lump-sum payment, the insurer provides the annuitant (you) with a guaranteed, fixed monthly income, starting right away.

If you are approaching retirement, though, now is the time to learn more about SPIAs.[2]

Choosing a life income annuity for retirement can be overwhelming. Insurers have typically based their annuity quotes on wildly divergent, often opaque, features—making the task of choosing annuities especially difficult. And in the face of so much information overload, many people simply give up—and end up knowing next to nothing about the great value of income annuities.

There is at least one web site where you can request competing quotes—on identical terms, so that the bids you get are truly comparable, apples-to-apples alternatives.[3] Currently, the Income Solutions platform is available through financial advisors and to account holders at Vanguard, though it would be a welcome improvement to see this kind of transparency become the new norm in the annuities market. (It's important to add that purchases made through Vanguard or advisors involve fees—and you should ask that these be disclosed to you clearly if you decide to pursue this avenue further.)

Choosing from the Annuity Menu

In order to request a meaningful bid, you need to know what's available—and what's right for you. It's a frustrating chicken-and-egg hurdle, but we can begin to overcome it with a simple overview of the principal decisions you'll need to make.

Simplicity rules. Stay with plain vanilla. Cut through the plethora of choices by taking the time to clarify what it is you most want and need. Remember that the extras you may be offered all come with a price. On further reflection, you may well decide that most of them are superfluous, so think carefully and then stick to your guns.

Single or Joint?

The first decision is whether to cover just yourself or yourself and your spouse. A joint-and-survivor life annuity will be more costly, but it will cover both spouses. A single life annuity will not pay out to your spouse after your death—unless you choose to have a guarantee period. (A guarantee period is finite, though, and it can be costly.)

Inflation Protection?

It's possible to buy an annuity with inflation protection. Because you're now familiar with the potential ravages inflation can inflict, you will want to consider this option very seriously. You'll almost certainly be floored when you first see the cost, but before you dismiss this protection as too expensive, be sure you understand how the cost compares with the benefits—and with the alternatives.

For a better appreciation of the benefits of inflation protection, think of what your income will buy in 20 years if it's not protected from inflation. Even if inflation is only "mild" for 20 years, recall that today's dollar will have the buying power of just 55 cents.

And consider your alternatives, too, for a helpful benchmark. Your alternative to an annuity is to invest the annuity's purchase price and gradually spend it down each year. How much income can you count on from such a portfolio? The most common rule of thumb for setting retirement withdrawal rates is to use a 4 percent guideline. If you retired with an investment portfolio of $100,000, for example, you'd withdraw an inflation-adjusted $4,000 each year.

An annuity quote for inflation-adjusted monthly income of $500 in exchange for a onetime payment of $100,000 translates to an inflation-adjusted $6,000 a year, and a withdrawal rate of 6 percent.

Consider the 4 percent benchmark only as a shorthand to give you perspective. In itself, it's just a rule of thumb—and a flawed one at that. If your investments are in stocks (and the rule-of-thumb portfolio generally has 60 percent of its holdings in stocks), then 4 percent is probably too high, especially if losses occur in the early years.

When comparing your annuity quote to a 4 percent withdrawal rate, bear in mind that the 4 percent rule-of-thumb withdrawal rate is not backed by an insurance company guarantee, and that it's generally applied not over a lifetime but to a 30-year horizon.

Finally, recognize that annuity rates fluctuate. The quotes you receive may have a short shelf life, so it's wise to base your final decisions on information that's very current.

Fixed Term or Life?

The risk of outliving your money should guide your decision. Patrick has been treating this decision as a gamble: Will I get a good deal from the insurance company or will they beat me? He's not alone. If you fall into his camp, try these two antidotes. First, don't gloss over the insurance value of an income for life. As you weigh your options, try widening your frame by imagining a penurious old age.

Second, it's possible to add a guarantee period, such as a 10-year certain period. That way, you can feel protected against mightily "overpaying" the insurance company if you die within 10 years. If you do die before the end of the time certain, your beneficiaries will still receive income for the full 10 years certain. Of course, as we've said, you will have to pay for this feature—but it may give you the comfort you seek.

Other ways to deal with longevity risk are scarce. Longevity insurance policies are available, although they are still relatively rare and do not usually come with inflation protection. They look a lot like their kissing cousins, deferred annuities, which provide a fixed future income stream in exchange for a lump-sum payment today. But neither of these typically offer inflation-protected income.

Choosing a Strong Insurer

It is vital to consider only the strongest insurers with reliable claims-paying capacity. Insurer strength has come to the fore as a serious issue in the wake of the financial instability we have experienced since 2008. To allay concerns about insurer claims-paying capacity, choose your provider with diligence and care.[4]

There are a number of criteria to consider. How long has the company been in this business? How strong is its balance sheet? What scores does it get from the rating agencies? A.M. Best is one good source for insurance company ratings.[5] For public companies, you can also consult the claims-paying ability ratings assigned by Moody's, S&P, and Fitch. It's best not to rely exclusively on a single source, but to develop a composite picture if you can.

Insurance companies are regulated at the state level, and it is important to know that each state has a life and health insurance company guaranty association to protect policy-holders and beneficiaries against an insurance company bankruptcy. Each state has a maximum liability that it will backstop, so be sure to check what that maximum level is in your state.[6] In case of bankruptcy, the association will either pay or transfer the claims to a solvent company.

Although state guaranty associations are no substitute for choosing a strong, stable insurer, they do offer some reassurance against potential insurance company failure. It's a good idea to stay below the maximum guarantee amount by parceling your annuity purchases among several providers.

Parceling your annuities in this way also lessens your exposure to any one insurance company. Times change—and spreading your exposure among several companies is a good way to mitigate the risk that comes even with strong insurers.

How Much to Annuitize?

For many people, this is the most perplexing question of all. To make it easier, you can adopt a staged strategy. By buying your annuities in "chunks," you'll accomplish several things. You'll match your annuitization schedule to your retirement plans—especially if, like many people today, you are planning to retire gradually. And a phased approach accords well with the parceling strategy for minimizing the risk of insurance company failure.

Finally, you'll free yourself of the scary burden of making a single, irrevocable lifetime decision. And you'll retain flexibility—both objectively and subjectively.

Calculating Your Income Gap

Once you've decided to think in stages, it becomes easier to name the amount of money you wish to annuitize. To keep you afloat during retirement, the monthly annuity payment should fill the gap between your retirement income and your fixed expenses. If you retire gradually, your reliable income stream will taper off gradually too, and you can annuitize your income gap in several smaller steps.

Notice that we've shifted our sights from the lump-sum payment to annual (or monthly) income in retirement. It's this income figure, and not some magic total wealth amount, that should become your measuring stick. As for the income gap—this is familiar ground that we've been over before. As you approach retirement, of course, you'll be able to refine your earlier estimates.

Continue to keep things simple. Update your personal goals map with the latest information, but don't be tempted to add excessive details or complexity.

Here is a thumbnail refresher to help speed you along. Think in terms of your major income categories—Social Security, income from transitional work, defined benefit pension income, bequests you will receive. Remember to include only income that you're sure of receiving. If you need the fingers of more than one hand to count your categories, you've gone too far. Stop and simplify.

On the expense side, consider the major nondiscretionary categories. Typical basic categories are food and shelter (including utilities), transportation, clothing, and medical expenses—which may now loom much larger than you once anticipated—and taxes.

Start by using the expenses that are truly nondiscretionary—the things you need and must have. This will lead you to your minimum necessary income gap. It's the income and lifestyle that cannot be put at risk.

If you are more risk averse, you can also calculate your expenses a second way, using your desired lifestyle spending and not simply your essential needs as your goal. Comparing the two numbers will give you a more concrete sense of how much risk you are prepared to take in order to achieve your aspirational wants. If you decide you want to ensure your current lifestyle, you'll place more of your investments in annuities and inflation-linked bonds.

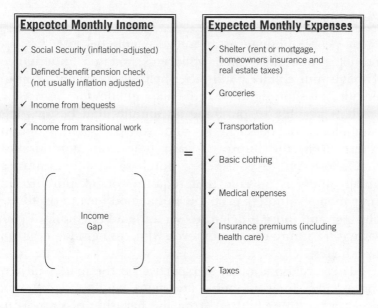

Figure 8.1   Do You Have a Retirement Income Gap?

When Can I Retire?

Your income gap calculation can also show you when you can afford to retire. Simply put, if you can see your way clear to buying an annuity to fill your coming income gap, you are within striking distance of a retirement you can afford.

Even if you remain unsure of when you will retire, you can buy smaller income annuities in series, as you gradually cut back on your working hours. By thinking in steps you can manage any uncertainty you have about your full retirement date.

Finally, if you are reading this section but are not thinking about retiring any time soon, use these guidelines to turbocharge your preretirement saving and investing so that you're not forced to keep working into your eighties. Scrutinize your current spending for nonessential expenses you can shift into savings. You may be surprised to find some current spending you can trade in for later enjoyment.

How Much for My Heirs?

Many people hesitate to annuitize mainly because they are unwilling to reduce their children's potential inheritance. Though your children and other heirs are certainly a consideration, it is short-sighted to rule out annuities for this reason.

It is possible to purchase an annuity that bestows left-over money on beneficiaries—but you pay for this option. Alternatively, the improved cash flow from annuitization may allow you to consider a purchase of life insurance. Finally, there is no rule that requires you to annuitize all your money—and it's probably not a good idea to do so. It's cheaper and more efficient to set aside a big chunk of your savings for future disposition even while you gradually annuitize the rest.

There is also another perspective on the matter of leaving a legacy for your heirs. For many families, it can be a great gift to free children from the hardship of supporting elderly parents whose money has run out. Many of us know families—maybe including your own—whose relatives outlived their resources and whose families had to step up to shoulder the financial burden along with the emotional one.

Just In Case: Insurance

Some retirement expenses can't be nailed down but have the potential to be ruinously large. Emergencies happen, health crises crop up, and long-term care can become necessary. Insurance, though it may be expensive, is the most prudent and efficient protection against these costly surprises. In the case of long-term care insurance, self-insuring can be so onerous that even expensive insurance is usually preferable.

When used together, insurance, annuities, and TIPS ladders can keep your standard of living safe during retirement. For additional help with the process of quantifying the plans in this chapter, there are good tools available online.[7] Check with this book's companion web site for up-to-date suggestions.

CHAPTER

Investing Safely for Education

The best investment you can make is in yourself.
—Warren Buffett

Sue and Julia are particularly eager to have a safe foundation they can rely on for their children's college education.

In 2008, both of them suffered a serious setback in their families' college savings plans when the U.S. economy took a hit. Sue's balances fell by 28 percent. Each of them believed they had taken disciplined and conservative steps to guarantee their kids a college education, and so it came as a nasty shock.

Sue was particularly chagrined by the losses because her account was supposed to grow safer as her son got older, and in 2008 he was nearing college age. It was an "age-based" plan that had pledged to shift into less risky assets as each student beneficiary neared college age.

Sue had plenty of company among investors in 2008. Not only is the concept of "target date" funds flawed to begin with, as we've noted before. In addition, in 2008, a large portion of college savings plans that advertised themselves as

139

age-based nevertheless had large stock holdings in accounts designated for teenagers.

As a result of this experience, both Sue and Julia are newly skeptical, but also newly receptive to finding a safer alternative.

Finding the right safe asset to fund education is challenging, though. Tuition inflation in the last 20 years has outstripped consumer price inflation by nearly 2 to 1. Average college tuition costs have climbed 92 percent in the last decade alone.

Though an investment in TIPS will keep up with general inflation, it's not guaranteed to match tuition increases. There are prepaid investment plans that ought to eliminate the risk of tuition inflation but are not necessarily sure bets. It helps that there are a number of tax-advantaged programs available for college investing. But it can be bewildering to sort through the patchwork quilt of programs and find the best combination of tax advantages and investments that are relatively safe.

To wade through the thicket, the simplicity mantra is invaluable. So we'll stick to basics. We'll focus first on safety and then weigh the advantages and limitations of the least risky investment options. The aim here is to sharpen your view of the landscape, with special emphasis on matching your goals with the safest suitable investment choices. There are several reasons that an expert advisor can be very helpful as you proceed.

Tax matters play an extremely important role, so your own individual circumstances will be unique, and this chapter can only provide you with a preliminary orientation. An expert advisor can help you review your individual situation in detail. But choose an advisor who has the background to evaluate an investment's impact on your eligibility for financial aid too. Just make sure the advisor you select shares a commitment to safe outcomes.

Capturing your goals requires imagination, and an expert advisor can be helpful here as well. Just as you included such wide-ranging elements as your career, your family, and your flexibility when you thought about retirement, you also want to cover a broad canvas when mapping your family's educational goals. What degree of responsibility will your child assume? How much can he or she be expected to contribute? What range of school types and locations will you consider? How much financial aid can you expect, and how much debt can your child handle? Are there grandparents who wish to contribute?

If you are starting early—and it makes sense to do so if you can—you won't be able to answer many of these questions for some time. But over time, they will help you to home in on your goals and to separate your aspirations from your essential requirements.[1]

I Bonds for Education

I Bonds are a reasonably good investment for college. They not only have tax advantages before they're redeemed but are entirely free of federal and most state tax when used for qualified education expenses.

This exemption is subject to phase-out based on income. Because the phase-out levels can change, we urge you to verify the current phase-out income range at the IRS web site.[2] Note, too, that this exemption only extends to owners who were older than 24 years at the time of purchase. Children who were given I Bonds in their names do not qualify.

Although I Bonds protect their holders from increases in the Consumer Price Index, their hedge with tuition inflation is far from perfect. The education exemption improves their appeal for those who qualify.

529 Prepaid Tuition Plans

A 529 plan is a tax-advantaged investment plan designated by Congress to encourage saving for education. Beneficiaries can be your children or grandchildren—or yourself, or any other individual you wish. These plans are administered by the states through state agencies and their partners in the private sector, making for a highly diverse array of possibilities. They have no income restrictions.

529 plans can be either savings plans or prepaid tuition plans. From the vantage point of safety, the prepaid tuition plans are a good place to begin, because they ostensibly should have a high capacity to hedge tuition inflation.

There are about a dozen state prepaid programs in existence. One or two have closed to new participants. In addition, a group of a few hundred private colleges offers the national Independent 529 Plan for students who attend one of its participating colleges.[3] Many of these plans offer the opportunity to lock in current tuition rates, if enrollees adhere to a stipulated contribution plan and time frame, which typically varies with the age of the student. Clearly, the fit is best for the student who is highly likely to attend a public college in the home state.

These plans are not without risk. Except for the national Independent 529 Plan, each is limited to its own state— although some plans do have provisions for transferring tuition credits to an out-of-state or private college. Exiting or canceling a plan can carry brisk penalties. All these terms bear careful scrutiny. Terms change, too, so try to stay current.

Some of the state plans are backed by state guarantees. But there is plenty of fine print, and at least one state guarantee—Alabama's—has not held up. The plans also face potential shortfalls as a result of economic stress.

In short, the prepaid option is one to consider carefully for its close hedge of tuition costs. But pay close attention to the risks and limitations.

529 Savings Plans

There is an even wider array of 529 savings plans. Cutting right to the chase, we suggest that you seek out the low-cost provider who also has a TIPS fund option. Don't get overwhelmed by this prospect, though—there are a few good calculators on the Internet that can help you weigh the alternatives fairly painlessly.[4] Plans that offer TIPS as an option are still limited to about a dozen.

You don't need to be a resident of the sponsor state to enroll. But make sure to consider state tax deductions when you are figuring your expense load. That's because some states—not all—allow a state tax deduction for contributions to a 529 savings plan, and this sometimes requires enrollment in your own state's plan. There is no federal tax deduction for 529 contributions.

As long as the money in a 529 account is used for a beneficiary's qualified education expenses, it will never be taxed. Contribution limits imposed by states are quite high—often $250,000 or even more. But it's a good idea to get some tax advice. You may run into gift tax issues if you exceed the annual gift tax limits—which can be doubled when a contribution to a beneficiary is made by both spouses.

Sound complicated? There's more: You can buy your plan from a broker, or you can buy direct. Generally, the broker's program comes with advice, but you pay dearly. In all cases, it's a good idea to understand the fees and expenses you will be charged. The range can be eye-popping.

Another choice you have is between age-based strategies and allocations that you dictate yourself. Age-based plans start out aggressive and pledge to shift gradually into a more conservative stance. They have not fared well and remain quite risky despite their promises, as Sue found out the hard way. We do not recommend them. Alternatively, you can dictate a "static" allocation among several available options—typically mutual funds.

Except for TIPS funds, the options available in 529 plans generally belong in your risky zone. This means that they are suitable for your aspirational goals and take a back seat to your strategies for meeting your basic educational needs.

TIPS

About a dozen 529 plans offer TIPS funds. You can choose how much of your account to allocate to each fund that is on offer. Although a TIPS fund can't hedge tuition increases, the link with inflation offers some protection. Key the amounts allocated to TIPS to your minimum education goals. Be sure to take account of other safe investments you've made for college that are outside your 529 account, such as I Bonds.

Tuition Indexing

The College Savings Bank has a tuition-linked CD that is available in the state 529 savings plans of Arizona and Nevada. This CD is also available on a taxable basis directly from the College Savings Bank. Amounts up to the deposit insurance maximum of $250,000 are backed by FDIC insurance. It earns interest at a variable rate linked to the cost of tuition, as determined by the College Board's Independent Colleges (IC) 500 index. Interest rates are reset once a year.

If your child does not go to college, the entire principal and interest at maturity can be used for any purpose at maturity. If the money is in a taxable account, there are no penalties.

The interest rate offered, though, is not as good a hedge as it seems at first blush—it's the tuition inflation rate *minus* an announced margin, and the rate is also capped out at an announced maximum. Lately, that margin has been 2.15 percent for CDs that extend for 5 years or longer, and a little more for shorter terms. Maturities are available from 1 to 22 years, so you can match maturities to the dates of your expected tuition bills.

Coverdell Education Savings Accounts

The Coverdell Education Savings Account (or ESA) is yet another tax-advantaged possibility. Its investment options are nearly limitless. Withdrawals may be used for all education levels, not just college. You may therefore invest directly in TIPS in such an account, or in a TIPS fund, without being subject to tax. Another advantage is that managing your investment expenses is straightforward.

You are permitted to fund both a Coverdell account and a 529 plan.

Contributions to Coverdell accounts are limited to just $2,000 each year. Eligibility is subject to phase-out beyond stated income limits—but the income triggers for phase-out are quite a bit higher than those governing the I Bond education exemption. Beneficiaries must be under 18 years old at the time of the contribution. Again, it's wise to stay current with changing income triggers by checking the IRS web site.

Coverdell contributions are not tax deductible, but their earnings are not taxed as long as the money is used for education when withdrawn. If you can't use the money for education, or don't withdraw all the money before the beneficiary reaches age 30, the account will be subject to tax (on earnings and gains) and to a penalty from the IRS as well.

What's the takeaway? It's feasible to build a low-risk foundation for your college investments—one that's large enough to meet your minimum requirements. Even though a perfect tuition hedge is elusive, there are ample inflation-linked and tax-advantaged options available. You don't have to let the broker orientation of many states' 529 plans push you mindlessly into an expensive, risky college investment plan.

Different goals call for different investment strategies. Investing for education has its own collection of tax incentives, opportunities, inflation expectations, and time frames that set it apart from retirement investing. Yet for all these differences, the basic safety-first, goal-oriented strategy works well for both.

CHAPTER

Choosing Risky Investments

If God wanted us to fly, he would have given us tickets.
—Mel Brooks

You may still have money left over after investing in enough safe assets to cover your basic needs. If so, you can venture into the world of risky investments. You can't count on your returns here—and may actually lose money. So these investments are appropriate for funding your desires that are beyond the basics—the ambitions you aspire toward but can do without.

You'll find plenty of risky assets with high expected returns to choose from. For the most part, though, these investments are unlikely to do well in hard times. And they can turn into losers at any time. The risk zone is a realm to enter with eyes wide open—and only if you can afford to lose. It's not a place to bet the lunch money.

In this chapter, we'll introduce you to a range of risky investments—and to stocks in particular. We'll also look at some basic strategies for success, concentrating on three

fundamental concerns—your risk level, your expenses, and
your market behavior.

How Much Risk Is Right?

By definition, risk will surprise you. So, once you step outside
the safer investment zone, it's unreasonable to think you can
dial risk up or down with close control over outcomes. Still,
there are broad strategies that can guide you in ratcheting
your overall risk levels (but not your results) higher or lower.

Most investment primers launch their discussions of risk
by pointing you toward diversification. As we've discussed,
diversification is an excellent, common-sense tactic for damp-
ening risk. By spreading risks into multiple baskets, you lower
the chances of ruin if any one among them crashes.

But diversification is not a panacea. Viewing your goals
and needs as liabilities and matching them with safe investments is a more reliable way to manage your overall investment risk.

Once you have covered your essentials through hedging
in your safety zone, it is not unreasonable to take significant
risk with part of the "extra" wealth available to invest. There
are many ways to do this—including leveraging an investment in a broadly diversified portfolio of stocks, buying a
"hot stock," investing in gold coins, or even buying lottery
tickets. Like a trapeze artist in a circus, if you have a strong
safety net, you can take bigger chances up in the air.

It Depends

In general, deciding how much risk to take—and in what
form—depends on two key considerations.

The first is how high you've set your basic risk thermo-
stat. If you have sized your safety zone conservatively, with
a generous estimation of your future needs, then you're in a
position to assume more risk when you step away from safety.

On the other hand, if you have skimped in specifying
your needs, but still plan to invest in stocks and other risky

assets, then you're well advised to moderate your risk level outside your safe investment zone.

Ask yourself how truthfully you've set your needs level. How far above the poverty line will your safety zone put you? How much of your current lifestyle are you willing to forego if your risky investments do not pan out?

The second consideration is your personal risk profile—a matter of both subjective attitudes and objective capacity to roll with market fluctuations. In general, the safer and more flexible your human capital, the more risk you can objectively bear. At the close of this chapter, we'll see how Sam, Patrick, Julia, and Sue have applied these two criteria in shaping their risky investment choices.

Diversification and Correlation

One way to judge how diversified different investments actually are is to observe how they have behaved in the past. The more closely the assets' returns have moved in tandem, the more closely they are *correlated.*

In theory, correlation can range all the way from perfect correlation, where asset values move in lockstep, to perfect negative correlation, which indicates that asset values move in precise counterpoint with one another. The more out of phase two assets are, the more their risks can be said to offset one another.

Recognize, though, that correlations can change over time. For example, stock and bond returns have exhibited positive correlation in some periods and negative correlation in others.

When you diversify your holdings of individual stocks, the effects of imperfect correlation are at work. If you hold a broad enough array of different stocks, you can get closer to approximating the whole stock market. The specific risks inherent in each company's stock can offset one another— when one goes up another may go down, because events affect companies in different ways.

What you cannot diversify away, though, is the risk of the market as a whole. When you hold a broad stock portfolio, this is where your risk—and your reward—will lie.

Index Funds

One of the most efficient ways to achieve diversification within an asset class is through index funds. An index fund is merely a mutual fund that owns shares in proportion to their representation in a market index—such as the S&P 500, an index of the 500 largest U.S. public companies—or the EAFE, an international index of stocks in the developed countries of Europe, Australia, and the Far East. Because index funds mirror an index benchmark rather than holding specially selected securities, they're called "passively" managed funds.

The case for indexing is compelling. Index funds have a long history of beating all but a small percentage of active managers over time. There is no guarantee that you can identify the highest-performing managers in advance. It's also rare for high performers to sustain market-topping returns for years on end.

Several studies have shown that much mutual fund outperformance is due to luck rather than skill—and is therefore not readily sustainable. Unfortunately, many individual investors avoid indexing because they're bent on beating the market. But they're probably wasting time and money chasing an illusion, because indexing is a more reliable option for the best returns over time.[1]

Asset Classes

You can also diversify your investments across different classes of assets. Asset classes are categories of securities or other assets that have similar features, behave in similar ways, and are governed by similar laws and regulations. The major core asset classes consist of equities (stocks), bonds, and money market (cash) instruments.

Asset allocation is a way to balance risk and reward by adjusting the proportion of each asset class in your portfolio, based on your goals and your capacity for risk. It is premised on the notion that different asset classes behave differently from one another in different circumstances.

Let's briefly survey the main classes of risky assets.

Bonds Think of bonds as loans where you, as bondholder, are the lender. In discussions of portfolio diversification, you'll often find bonds featured prominently. But our safe-goal approach has limited use for bonds in the risky part of a portfolio. That's principally because TIPS and I Bonds form the core of your safety zone. There is little diversification value to add from other kinds of riskier bonds.

As we've seen, nominal Treasury bonds may be default free, but they don't protect you from inflation. They're potentially valuable in deflationary times, but we don't recommend them otherwise. The same is true for U.S. government agency bonds, which are also nominal bonds.

What about corporate bonds? A corporate bondholder is exposed to both default and inflation risk. If you're comfortable with the company's credit, then why not own the company's stock—you stand to be better rewarded. The diversification benefits of owning corporate bonds are not sufficient to tip the scales.

The one exception to this generalization is tax-exempt debt—*provided* that you are in a high income-tax bracket and expect to remain there for a long time. For high tax bracket individuals, the tax advantages can sometimes make municipal and other tax-exempt debt an attractive choice.

But buyers beware. This is not an easy time for our states and cities, nor is it ever a cakewalk for a nonexpert to peel back all the hidden complexities implicit in these bonds—and bond funds. Bond ratings are a good place to begin—but these are quite fallible.

Domestic Equities Consider anchoring your stock portfolio in the United States. As long as you plan on doing your spending in U.S. dollars, you're minimizing currency risk. And because so many U.S. companies do business abroad, you are also picking up some benefits of international diversification.

You can find low-cost index funds that own the whole U.S. stock market, including companies of all sizes. If you prefer to manage your exposure to smaller companies, which are typically riskier than larger firms, then you can choose separate index funds for large and small companies, and weight them according to your risk barometer.

International Equities To achieve greater diversification, add international equities to the mix. In today's globalizing economy, international equities make sense. Don't limit yourself to U.S. stocks—they represent a shrinking fraction of the world market.

Vanguard offers a one-stop-shop world index fund, which includes the United States along with all-world international markets. And there are whole-world international funds that exclude the United States as well. Or you can select separate funds for the developed world and emerging markets. Emerging markets extend the promise of higher expected growth—but with correspondingly high levels of risk.

For a short list of domestic and international index funds with low expense ratios, consult Table 10.1.

Real Estate It is important to distinguish between owning your own home, investing directly in other property, and investing in real estate investment trusts.[2] REITs are entities that invest in different kinds of real estate—including shopping centers, office buildings, hotels, and mortgages secured by real estate.

An advantage often touted for real estate investing is that it is not closely correlated with stocks or bonds. But real estate failed to zig when the market zagged—and sagged—in

Table 10.1   Selected Stock Index Funds with Low Expense Ratios

Fund Family	Description	Name and Symbol	Index	Expense Ratio*
Vanguard	USA: Large Company Stocks. Tracks the value of stocks of 500 of the largest companies, spanning many industries.	500 Index Fund (VFINX)	S&P 500	0.17%
Fidelity	USA: Large Company Stocks. Tracks the value of stocks of 500 of the largest companies, spanning many industries.	Spartan 500 Index Fund (FUSEX)	S&P 500	0.10%
Vanguard	USA Small and Mid-sized Company Stocks: Tracks 4,000 small and mid-sized companies. Index is considered a complement to the S&P 500	Extended Market Index Fund (VEXMX)	S&P Completion Index	0.30%
Fidelity	USA Small and Mid-sized Company Stocks: Index tracks stocks of some 4,500 small and mid-sized companies and excludes stocks in the S&P 500.	Spartan Extended Market Index Fund (FSEMX)	Dow Jones U.S. Completion Total Stock Market Index	0.10%
Vanguard	USA Total Stock Market: Index is designed to give exposure to the entire market including the stocks of small, mid- and large-size companies	Total Stock Market Index (VTSMX)	MSCI U.S. Broad Market Index	0.18%
Fidelity	USA Total Stock Market: Index is designed to give exposure to the entire market including the stocks of small, mid- and large-size companies	Spartan Total Market Index Fund (FSTMX)	Dow Jones U.S. Total Stock Market Index	0.10%

(Continued)

Table 10.1 Selected Stock Index Funds with Low Expense Ratios (Continued)

Fund Family	Description	Name and Symbol	Index	Expense Ratio*
Vanguard	International Stocks, Developed World ex U.S.: Index tracks over 1,000 company stocks in more than 20 developed countries in Europe and the Pacific Rim	Developed Markets Index Fund (VDMIX)	MSCI EAFE	0.22%
Fidelity	International Stocks, Developed World ex U.S.: Index tracks over 1,000 company stocks in more than 20 developed countries in Europe and the Pacific Rim	Spartan International Index Fund (FSIIX)	MSCI EAFE	0.20%
Vanguard	International Stocks: Emerging Markets. Index tracks approximately 750 companies in 21 emerging market countries	Emerging Market Stock Index Fund (VEIEX)	MSCI Emerging Market Index	0.35% + 0.50% purchase fee
Vanguard	International Stocks in Developed and Emerging Markets	Total International Stock Index Fund (VGTSX)	MSCI All-Country World ex U.S. Investable Market Index	0.26%
Vanguard	U.S. and International: Large and mid-cap stocks around the world including U.S., developed and emerging markets	Total World Stock Index Fund (VTWSX)	FTSE All-World Index	0.45% + 0.25% purchase fee

*Subject to change. Check prospectus.

2008. A second claim you often hear is that real estate helps hedge inflation. But the collapse of the real estate market in 2008 demonstrates how risky it is to rely on real estate values, regardless of inflation.

TIAA offers a real estate investment vehicle that provides individual investors with direct ownership of large pools of properties. Or, you can select a passive index vehicle offered by Vanguard.[3] The index tracks publicly traded REITs. There are others—as well as some passive exchange-traded funds (ETFs)— available too. But don't choose these investments for safety.

Other "Alternative" Investments There is a wide range of non-core, or "alternative" investments. For the most part, these are highly volatile and not a good choice for lay investors.

We're talking about venture capital, hedge funds, and even commodities. Commodities have held some allure for investors seeking a haven from the stock market's ups and downs. In general, commodities exhibit high volatility. Precious metals—and gold in particular—can be especially volatile. If you decide to invest in one of these alternatives, do so in moderation, and investigate carefully beforehand.

Controlling Costs

Keeping your investment expenses low is an easy way to boost your return without adding risk. It doesn't take special insight to see that high investment costs eat into your gains—but investors continually fall into the "luxury trap," believing that high fees signal high quality. Over time, the opposite is true, because high fees—which compound—will make you poorer.

Expense Ratios

An additional advantage of passive index funds is their extremely low expense ratio—the reduction in rate of return you give up—generally measured in basis points, or one-hundredths of a percentage point. Fund expenses vary widely from as little as 10 basis points for some index funds to as much as 300 basis points for some actively managed funds.

Another low-cost option is the exchange-traded fund, or ETF, a relative newcomer. As we've seen for ETFs that specialize in TIPS, these funds are baskets of securities but they trade like individual stocks. They can be bought and sold in real time, at any time that the market is open.

Each ETF purchase or sale generates a commission charge, although many companies will waive these fees under certain circumstances, so it is worth checking before you create an account.

Don't assume that all ETFs automatically have low expense ratios, or that they represent broadly diversified offerings. ETFs started out as index-type instruments for the most part—but actively managed, high-fee ETFs have proliferated as ETFs have begun to catch on. Some actively managed ETFs are highly levered and quite risky.

Tax Efficiency

It's a good idea to manage all your investments in a way that keeps your tax bills as low as possible. This includes paying attention to the location where you hold different assets. If you hold investments in a tax-deferred account, you can ignore income taxes on interest or dividend income or on realized capital gains as long as the money is in the account.

Some accounts that don't qualify for current tax deductions won't ever be taxed. This is the case for Roth IRAs and 529 or Coverdell accounts that are used for qualified education expenses. But retirement accounts such as traditional IRAs, 401(k)s, and 403(b) accounts will eventually be taxed on withdrawal—at future tax rates that are uncertain today.

It's smart to place your highest-taxed investments in tax-deferred accounts. As a general rule of thumb, tax efficiency for most people dictates that you place your TIPS and other interest-paying investments in tax-deferred accounts to the extent possible, and hold your equities in taxable accounts.

This is because interest is taxed as ordinary income.[4] Capital gains are taxed at a lower rate—just 15 percent today. Any gain you achieve by selling a stock after owning it for at least one year is taxed at the lower capital gains rate. You also get to claim some tax relief when you sell stocks at a loss—but you lose the benefit of both these advantages in a tax-deferred account. When you ultimately do withdraw your money from your tax-deferred accounts, it will be taxed as ordinary income.

For your taxable accounts, choose tax-efficient funds to the extent possible. Index funds and ETFs in particular are relatively tax-efficient. For investors in high income-tax brackets, there are tax-managed index funds that are worth looking into. Vanguard, for example, offers tax-managed funds with low expense ratios.

Finally, it's a good practice to do some tax planning at the start of each year—and to be aware that changes in the tax law are always possible.

Curb Your Enthusiasm

The third concern to bear in mind when investing in risky assets is human nature, and irrational behavior in particular.

In combating overconfidence and excessive optimism, it helps to have a straightforward plan and stick with it. That means avoiding excessive trading. Hyperactive buying and selling by individuals is costly. Not only do you rack up high transaction costs this way, but there is no evidence that anyone has the clairvoyance to time markets.

It's a good idea to be as reflective—not reflexive—as possible when you choose your investments. If you're not indexing, know why. And even if you don't trade often, avoid chasing yield by running after last year's hottest, best performing mutual fund. It's a losing proposition, though it's sadly widespread.

If you enjoy playing the stock market for entertainment, then pry your recreational goals apart from the rest and keep them in their own separate "bucket." This is a psychological move that lets you frame your pastime as a cost center rather than a profit machine—and it can help keep your play accounts appropriately small. To paraphrase Paul Samuelson: If you must sin, sin only a little. And be sure you can afford to invest for sport. Don't rob your safety zone and your standard of living.

No one is immune from irrational behavior. It's helpful to keep your plan in writing. Jot down your investment activity, along with brief justifications for your decisions, and then reread frequently to banish magical thinking and overconfidence.

Finally, unless you are highly motivated and diligent about your investing, consider working with a financial advisor. In the next chapter, we'll talk more about how to choose an advisor—and how not to end up with the wrong person who leads you down a garden path filled with thorns.

Sam Learns to Take More Risk

Let's look at the decisions that Julia and her colleagues have made after reflecting on what they've learned.

As far as their risk perspectives go, Sam and Patrick are quite the odd couple. Sam, still single and not yet 40, has become an unusually conservative investor. As you may remember, though, his friends judged his risk capacity to be moderate or higher—largely because of his work flexibility and his substantial earnings expectations.

Paradoxically, by studying his ability to reach his goals through safe investments—and grasping that most of his wealth will come from his earnings over the next 30 years— Sam has actually grown more comfortable taking some risk.

What was Paul's rationale for encouraging Sam to take more risk? If Sam is able to meet his minimum needs using safe investments, why take risk at all?

The answer is twofold. First, Sam is still in the process of formulating his aspirational goals. He's a bit clearer on his rock-bottom minimum needs, but there is a vast amount of information Sam still does not have—when he'll marry, whether he'll have children, whether he'll buy a house any time soon, and even what steady-state lifestyle he'll have in this, his new location.

And second, Sam has the objective capacity to bear some risk, considering his career flexibility, his professional growth expectations, and his relative youth. But his human capital can't be considered really secure, so he'll stay away from high risk.

Sam likes the advice he was given—to create a small reserve that he can expand and repurpose over time as he makes more life decisions—and has decided to set up a special war chest for the future. Right now, he's able to make large contributions, but he expects that may change as he makes major purchases and lifestyle choices in coming years.

Sam has set retirement goals in similarly rough fashion, choosing to contribute the maximum allowed by his employer's retirement plan. (His employer's matching contributions along with the tax advantages have motivated him.)

Sam has used these rough estimates of his future needs and aspirations to decide how large his safety zone should be for now. His choices have resulted in an overall allocation of 50 percent to risky assets. That allocation emerged after the fact—it was not based on arbitrary percentages or on a 50-50 product pulled from the shelf.

Now that he has a comfortable safety zone, Sam can decide how volatile his risky portfolio can be. Sam's ample human capital and his large safety zone both permit him to assume a fair amount of risk there. But by temperament—and because of his fear of a future layoff—he is sticking with moderate risk. With advice from Paul, he's decided to keep things as simple and balanced as possible, at least until he grows more accustomed to his new investing style.

In his taxable accounts, he's going to build up roughly equal positions in a total stock market index for domestic exposure and a total international index.

In his tax-deferred account, he will concentrate on the TIPS index fund offered by his employer's plan. He'll also add a small allocation there (not more than 5 percent) to a REIT index fund. The REIT fund adds further diversity to his risky portfolio—and the tax-deferred account is a suitable location for it, because REIT fund distributions are taxed as ordinary income.

Sam briefly considered boosting his risk by adding an investment in a technology fund, but rejected this idea when he realized he'd be expanding his exposure to the sector he works in. He's also planning to accumulate I Bonds gradually, aiming to make them the centerpiece of his emergency stash.

Patrick Puts on the Brakes

Patrick is Sam's nearly polar opposite: Nearing the end of his professional career, with only a little work flexibility, he nevertheless remains a big risk taker, and is only reluctantly coming to terms with the hardships he may face if his risky investments take another hit. He's done the same calculations as Sam, and realizes that he could well come up short. His earnings and savings in the next 10 to 12 years will be critically important in setting his standard of living during retirement.

So he's going to adopt a two-pronged strategy—he plans to work longer and save more each year. He'll have Marianne's backing in spending less. She'll also coordinate her retirement date with his. Because she's a little younger than Patrick, she'll try to work for a few years longer to ease their transition into retirement. Although Patrick is enthusiastic about the prospect of launching an encore career, he can't include any of its income in his plan. He'll have to demonstrate some success first.

To be sure he can cover his basics in retirement, Patrick will begin transitioning his investments into the safety of

TIPS. Marianne will coordinate her retirement plan investments with Patrick—and by the time they retire, they expect this strategy to lead them to an overall risky allocation of just about 25 percent. They're planning to annuitize part of their safe portfolio in stages, starting just before retirement, and will build a TIPS ladder that gives them enough liquidity when they retire to do so.

As for his stock portfolio, Patrick plans to keep its risk moderate—at least until he grows more confident that their safety zone is big enough to protect their retirement lifestyle. He is going to choose one fund, the Total World Stock Index, to keep himself away from temptation—even though the expenses he'll shoulder will be a bit higher than if he were to pick a selection of index funds with less individual breadth.

Because his 401(k) does not yet have a TIPS option, Patrick will have to find a different location for his TIPS investments. He has a relatively large rollover IRA where he can start adding 10-year TIPS to build a ladder. Marianne has an opportunity at work to invest in a TIPS fund through TIAA.

Sue Wonders Whether to Shoot the Moon

As Sue reviewed her goals, she realized that she has a lot less slack than she had once thought. Despite her good income, and her safe, flexible human capital, her educational goals are looming. Adding further strain on her budget, her fixed household expenses are high and her ability to save is smaller than she'd like. Now that she's on her own, Sue has made the prudent decision to increase her life insurance policy, but the bigger premium payments also put pressure on her ability to save.

In her educational "silo," Sue is going invest 100 percent of her savings in safer assets. She doesn't have an extremely long time to accumulate savings. In addition, she has little confidence that her ex will come through with extra help for college and doesn't have the resilience to withstand a big dip in the value of her investments.

In the short run, Sue may have to reduce her retirement plan contributions to accommodate her education saving. But she doesn't plan to quit her retirement investing altogether. Her contributions have the double effect of lowering her current tax bill and building up her retirement balances. Also, she knows that her retirement account balances—such as 401(k)s and IRAs—do not count for purposes of calculating federal financial aid for education.

Sue is debating how much risk she can afford to take in her retirement account. She wants to argue for more risk, especially because she expects to contribute for another 20 years, and because her income is quite secure.

And she has a particular risky investment in mind. For some time, she has been thinking about investing a chunk of her retirement savings in her friends' early-stage company. She's highly confident in both their venture and their abilities—and she was pleased to learn from Paul that a narrow, undiversified, and rather risky investment was not necessarily irresponsible as long as her safe investments covered her well enough.

But she appreciates that this undiversified, private investment is quite speculative. It could result in outsize gains, but it could also produce extreme loss—and Sue has begun to vacillate.

In order to decide, Sue has to judge whether her safe retirement investments are substantial enough to comfortably cover her goals or not. She has asked Paul to help her review her budget numbers and income projections and finally concludes that her safety threshold is lower than she'd ideally want. Under her current assumptions, she's barely going to cover her retirement essentials, even though they are so far in the future.

So she's going to stick with a larger safety zone, putting just 50 percent of her retirement savings into stocks instead of the larger amount she had been contemplating. She'll also drop her private investment opportunity, and will instead assume only moderate risk in her equity portfolio.

To keep matters clear and simple, she's going to invest in two index funds—a total market domestic stock index fund and an all-country world (except the U.S.) index fund.

Julia Invests Her Inheritance

Julia has used her new knowledge to break out of her paralysis and decide what to do with her inheritance. Paul's emphasis on goals and their underlying values have been especially helpful in getting her going.

Julia is glad that Paul emphasized the value of consulting with her husband Jim during the decision process. Jim opened her mind to new possibilities she had not considered before, and she's more confident in her choices as a result of his support. In retrospect, she can hardly believe that she hadn't included him in her deliberations from the outset. Instead, she'd wasted time listening to her two brothers try to win her over to a plan she disliked.

By rethinking her goals aloud, Julia has grown newly aware that family, independence, and professional satisfaction are among her topmost values. For Julia, these translate into three key financial goals: a good education for her children, a fulfilling and productive career for herself, and a retirement with Jim that will be comfortable enough to let them enjoy their family well into the future, without having to worry about becoming dependent.

Because Julia and Jim have no immediate call for the money she has inherited—no major loans to pay off, no impending big expenses—they are free to be guided by Julia's goals.

She has decided to divide the inheritance in three.

She plans to put a third of it into her business—something she hadn't considered until Jim suggested it. She'd thought it too risky, especially in a difficult economic climate. But, with Jim's encouragement—and after learning to appreciate the role of work income in building wealth—she began to devise a targeted investment plan for her business.

She has identified a few high-impact opportunities for her firm: She will most likely upgrade her equipment, her computing technology, and her demonstration gardens—and she'll put resources into social media, advertising, and her Web presence as well. Using I Bonds, she'll also set aside a small fund to keep her training up-to-date through conferences and seminars in future years.

Her aims are to sustain her professional success and satisfaction—and to build wealth over time.

She'll take another third of the inheritance to pay down part of the mortgage on their home. She settled on this plan after she and Jim sat down to examine their fixed household expenses—and realized that paying down part of the mortgage would free up more money for discretionary spending (and saving) for the next 18 years of the mortgage term, as well as making it easier to ride out any temporary downturns in her income.

The last third she'll invest, dividing the money between safe and risky investments. Julia wants to buy TIPS—but she'd like to buy more than she is allowed this year in any of her tax-advantaged accounts.

Julia has a way around this obstacle. Like many of us, her existing tax-deferred accounts evolved somewhat haphazardly and are not especially tax-efficient. They include a large allocation to equity funds. Julia's solution is to move out of these investments and into TIPS in her tax-deferred account, with a big overall improvement in tax efficiency.

Because she has a tax-deferred brokerage account, she can buy a combination of TIPS funds and individual TIPS bonds. She can then use her new money to buy risky investments in her taxable accounts. (The amount of new money is about the same as the tax-deferred TIPS purchases, so she'll end up with a roughly even split between them.)

Unlike Sue, Julia thinks she can comfortably cover her children's education expenses because she is starting early. The same is true for retirement. Her earnings profile is flexible, her husband's income is relatively stable, and they are able to save enough money each year to cushion her from any sudden fluctuation in her business income. They have a good tax-deferred location from which to build a TIPS ladder and they have a long horizon in which to do it.

Because Julia's safety zone is also on firm ground, she has moderate to high risk capacity in her risky zone and can tilt her risky investments a little more to the volatile side than her friends can. This tilt will be more pronounced for retirement than for education, given how far along they are in their retirement investing.

Like her peers, Julia will choose passive index funds. She'll buy the S&P 500, a large-cap domestic index fund, and will add a small cap index fund (of small capitalization U.S. stocks). Because she's buying it for her taxable account, she's selected a tax-managed small-cap index fund. To this she'll add exposure to world stocks, in both the developed and emerging markets. She's decided not to add exposure to REITs because her livelihood is so closely tied to the real estate market.

You can borrow the methods that Julia, Sam, Patrick, and Sue have used. Start with your goals, consider how much you can save each year to meet them, and use your human capital profile to help guide your path.

CHAPTER

11

How to Choose an Advisor

First, do no harm.

—Origin uncertain

Do you need a financial advisor?

As with all services you shop for, it's useful to decide first on the scope of advice you're seeking. Chances are that you're not just looking for a narrow set of investment recommendations. It's more likely that you want a hand in setting your destinations, guiding your tax planning, and more.

You may want direction in separating your needs from your wants. Or you may be looking for assistance in making realistic estimates of your future expenses, based on the career and income trajectory you envisage.

Let's face it—this work is all too easy to postpone. Having a trustworthy, knowledgeable advisor would make it much easier to get the job done. Not to mention the extra support you'd get in positioning your plans for a comfortable retirement. After age 50, expert advice can be particularly valuable.

Perhaps most importantly of all, an advisor can be the trusted counselor who helps you clarify—at various stages of your life—where to place your risk set point and when to change it.

Because these decisions are so vital, a bad choice could be costly. But the path to a trustworthy, capable advisor is anything but clear. Many people who want guidance with their planning and investing remain stuck at the gateway. Or they end up making do with a broker they once struck up with, in a happenstance way, but who may not really suit their needs at all.

And it's no wonder. The profession encompasses a confusing jumble of salesmen, portfolio managers, and investment counselors. It's in this last category of counseling that you'll find the most enduring value.

Julia, Sam, Patrick, and Sue got lucky. They had a low-risk opportunity to spend a few months with Paul and to educate themselves about money, risk, and investing. Most people don't get this chance. So this chapter will try to help fill the gap. It's designed as an enhanced checklist to equip you with some resources and radar in your search—and to help you avoid players whose interests are not well aligned with your own.

Getting Started

A good place to begin is with referrals from trusted friends and family. It's important to treat all referrals as a prelude to more questions, though. Some of the worst horror stories of fraud and scams came about because the victims took recommendations on pure faith.

You can also find the names of advisors in your area on the web sites of NAPFA, the National Association of Personal Financial Advisors, and of FPA, the Financial Planning Association.[1]

Treat your list as a starting point for further exploration. After all, you're looking for an enduring relationship based on mutual respect and trust, so plan on investing at least as much effort as you'd put into choosing an automobile.[2]

Screening for the Right One

Not all advisors have your best interests at heart. The recent Madoff fraud is just one recent, if unforgettable, reminder. But many advisory practices that are completely legal can still be harmful to your well-being.

As long ago as 1940, ex-Wall Streeter Fred Schwed published a hilarious, barbed profile of the investment business, which he called *Where Are the Customers' Yachts?* The title was a nod to an old Wall Street joke about an out-of-town visitor who was guided around town and shown some impressive yachts. When told he was seeing the bankers' and brokers' fine boats, the visitor naively pressed on: Where were the customers' yachts, he wanted to know.

Today, the figure of the broker who gets rich at the customers' expense remains entirely familiar. "The Wrong Financial Advisor" is a side-splitting YouTube lampoon created by Nobelist William Sharpe that you can't afford to miss if you are searching for an advisor.[3]

After watching Sharpe's video, you'll be impressed with the urgency of screening advisors hard for hype and magical thinking. Remember the adage that if it seems too good to be true, it almost certainly is.

Wharton finance professor Kent Smetters, who has been working to bring affordable financial advisory services to a wider audience, suggests three key questions for screening out the wrong type of advisor. He suggests that you focus on commissions, fees, and whether the advisor has pledged to act at all times as your fiduciary—placing your interests first and adhering to the highest standards of client care.[4]

Commissions

Commissions are commonly paid on investment products, annuities, and insurance. There is nothing inherently wrong with them. Potential problems arise, though, when the professionals you turn to for financial advice are brokers, paid by third parties for making a sale. Many brokers call themselves financial advisors, so names don't necessarily tell you all you need to know. Nor is "independence" a sign of objectivity. Just because advisors are independent does not mean that they don't receive commissions (or referral fees) from third parties. You have to ask.

Commissions are problematic in this context for two reasons. First, they take more money out of your pocket than you may need to spend. Often, commissions are not transparent, but invisibly embedded in the total that you invest—as in the case of secondary market TIPS, which were discussed in Chapter 7—and in the case of individual bonds in general. Advice offered "for free" often comes from salespeople whose products have commissions embedded in them.

A second problem with commissions is the basic conflict of interest they create when the broker is acting as your investment advisor. It's in the broker's interest to make the sale, whether the product is best for you or not. Even upright, highly ethical brokers are subject to this conflict, which can operate at a subconscious level.

Fee-Only Compensation

By contrast, a fee-only compensation arrangement minimizes conflicts of interest. But be sure you ask for, and get, a compensation structure that is fee-only, and *not* simply fee-based. Fee-based advisors can switch back and forth between planning fees and commissions when they are dual-registered advisors, so beware.

Fee-only advisors can structure their fees on a retainer basis, or as a fee for service—for example, a flat fee for a financial check-up—or as a percentage of assets under management (which is most common). Some advisors and planners also have hourly rates, although this option has become less usual.

Although these formulas are all acceptable, the assets-under-management model can sometimes contain hidden pitfalls that a flat fee or hourly rate don't share. It creates an incentive for the advisor to grow your assets to mutual advantage, but it sometimes leads advisors to steer you toward extra risk, or toward oversaving. (Yes, there is such a thing!) For example, the advisor may talk you out of buying insurance products that would lower your risk but reduce the amount of your investments under management. These are matters you can clarify in your interview.

Client First

Your interests are best served by an advisor who is also a *fiduciary*. Legally, a financial advisor who is held to a fiduciary standard is required to act with undivided loyalty to the client, placing the client's interests ahead of its own at all times. A fiduciary must disclose how the advisor is compensated along with any related conflicts of interest.

Fiduciary Principles

The Committee for the Fiduciary Standard was formed by concerned professionals in 2009 to advocate for holding all advisors to the "authentic fiduciary standard" (as established under the Investment Advisors Act of 1940) and to ensure broad access for investors to advice that is truly in their best interest.

The Committee has distilled the fiduciary standard into five core fiduciary principles, which are essential:

- Put the client's best interest first
- Act with prudence; that is, with the skill, care, diligence, and good judgment of a professional
- Do not mislead clients; provide conspicuous, full, and fair disclosure of all important facts
- Avoid conflicts of interest; and
- Fully disclose and fairly manage, in the client's favor, unavoidable conflicts.

Source: The Committee on the Fiduciary Standard, in its announcement of the Tamar Frankel Fiduciary Award, http://www.bu.edu/phpbin/news-cms/news/?dept=634&id=57703

Investment advisors and broker-dealers are regulated under different regulatory regimes. The Dodd-Frank Wall Street Reform and Consumer Protection Act of 2010 authorized (but did not require) the Securities and Exchange Commission to impose a uniform fiduciary standard of care for brokers and advisors. As of the first anniversary of the legislation, though, the SEC has not yet done so. But it has completed a study and has, at the start of 2011, recommended that the fiduciary standard of care be applied to all financial advisors who provide investment advice about securities to retail investors.

So do watch out for dual-registered advisors. They can shift in and out of fiduciary status as they exchange their financial-planner hats for those of a broker. Nonfiduciary broker-dealers and their registered representatives are held to the lower standard of suitability, which allows them to offer only "suitable" advice, even if they are aware that it isn't the best advice for their client. Under the suitability standard, an advisor could, for example, recommend a mutual fund that returned a fee to the advisor—even if the advisor knew that a comparable, less expensive fund was available.

Interviewing Candidates

Plan to interview at least three candidates. Find out an advisor's qualifications, experience, credentials, and licenses. Remember, you're the one with a job to fill. It's your turn to sit in the interviewer's chair. If you like, bring your interview notes with you to your meeting.[5]

Scope of Service

Ask, too, about the scope of services the advisor can provide. As investment consultant and author Charley Ellis has recently pointed out, it is in the realm of comprehensive investment counseling—and not narrow portfolio management—that financial advisors can add enduring value.

There are important advantages to working with an advisor who can help you with insurance and even estate planning, and who has an integrated understanding of your whole life.

If the advisor does not offer comprehensive services—including estate and tax planning, for example—find out how they expect to get a whole picture of you. And ask how they coordinate their advice with other professionals who advise you—because you're hoping to simplify your life, not make it more complex. Finally, be sure that they will provide you with a personal investment policy statement and a plan that incorporates it.

Approach: Goals and Risk

When discussing an advisor's approach to investing, concentrate on the closely allied issues of goals and risk. Expect to spend some time on these subjects.

Ask how the advisor will integrate your goals with your investments. It's the rare advisor who doesn't offer at least lip service to the centrality of your goals. But not all advisors make your goals the driver of your investment plan. Yet, as readers of this book will recognize, a goals-based approach is the surest route to your destinations.

Ask, too, about their approach to risk. Do they define risk as volatility? Or do they see it in a more personalized light, as the chance you may miss your goals? The answers are worth pursuing, because they're likely linked with an advisor's basic philosophy and risk management strategies. Do the advisors rely exclusively on diversification? Or do they use safer investments to help make sure that you reach your goals? Be sure their answers are clear. One way to get at this is to require that the advisor provide you with two plans: a minimum risk plan and an average risk plan.

One common mantra to watch out for is that you *have to* take on more risk or else you *can't* reach your goals. That's a misstatement that can cost you heavily. Or you may encounter a related reaction—outright hostility to safer investments—including a blanket repudiation of TIPS as a "way to make you poorer." Such attitudes devalue the role

of insurance and predictability in ensuring your goals at
their minimum, basic level.

Chemistry

Your intuition counts, of course—but only in light of your
due diligence. Once you've qualified your candidates,
your personal comfort level is extremely important. Part of
the equation includes an advisor's explanatory skills—which
are distinct from powers of persuasion. It's important that
you understand the advice you are receiving very clearly.
What about listening ability? Even while you are interview-
ing them, you're probably getting some sense of how well
they are actually hearing you.

In short: The best advisor will understand your situation and can fit your investment plan to you, while explain-
ing things clearly. Look for someone who is a professional
counselor first and foremost, and not just a businessman-
investor—to borrow a key distinction recently highlighted
by author Charley Ellis.[6]

More Homework

In addition to your interviews, be sure to request—and
read—each advisor's ADV to find out that everything checks
out. You'll also learn whether he or she has had problems
with regulators (or clients). The SEC describes Form ADV
as "the uniform form used by investment advisers to register
with both the Securities and Exchange Commission (SEC)
and state securities authorities."[7]

There are also web sites you can check to verify accredi-
tations and licenses, as well as to check the disciplinary history of a financial planner or advisor.[8] We've listed the top
sites in the notes to this chapter.

And, if you are up for it, there is more research you can
do. Check the end notes for a few suggestions.[9]

Epilogue

O brave new world . . .

—William Shakespeare

Some encouraging changes are afoot in the world of personal finance. Spurred by the imminent retirement of the Baby Boomer generation—and by the notable volatility of markets in this new century— a new emphasis on risk management is gathering force. The influence of Boomer retirement on the investment landscape can't be overstated. It is expected to span the next 20 years or longer and to involve some 77 million people, about 1 in 4 Americans.

And the market experience of the past decade has hammered home the realization that catastrophes can be larger, more frequent, and more disruptive than conventional expectations suggest.

Also part of the same trend is a widening acceptance of the safety-first principle: Start planning for retirement by building a safe minimum or floor, and if there is money left over, take on exposure to risk. Cover the basics and only then "go for upside."[1]

Along with this incipient shift in perspective, there is also growing appetite among investors for products that offer downside protection along with the potential for gain—a way to have your cake and eat a piece of it, too.

Both this demand and the growing acceptance of safety-first principles grow out of two warring sentiments: a lifetime of loving stocks and a fervent desire to avoid more loss.

Many financial advisors and educators have told their clients that before they start investing in risky assets, they should make sure they've taken care of their needs for insurance—life insurance, disability insurance, home and auto insurance, health insurance, and, eventually, long-term care insurance. Paradoxically, many of those same advisors have also told their clients that if they are saving and investing for the long run, they can rest assured that there is little risk in the stock market.

As a result, many Boomers hold retirement portfolios that are far riskier than they think. Yet Boomers, who have grown up with a fine appreciation of the value of insurance, are also receptive to the notion of insuring against the risk in their portfolio.

There are basically two ways to insure against the downside of the stock market: trade some of the stocks that you own for inflation-protected bonds matched in maturity to your target spending dates, or buy protective put options on your stock portfolio. The first method guarantees a minimum level of inflation-protected income; the second limits the potential loss in the value of your stock portfolio.

We've talked a great deal about the first of these alternatives. Let's look now at the second. An option is an instrument that gives its holder the right to buy (if it is a call) or sell (if it is a put) an asset for a specified ("strike") price within a particular time period. If the asset doesn't reach the strike price before the option expires, then nothing happens—and the holder is out just the price of the option.

But if you own a stock index fund or ETF along with a put for that index, you have effectively created a form of insurance. You have set a floor value for your asset. If the value of the index you own falls below the strike price, you are protected. You get to sell it at the strike price. At the same time, you get to hold on to any gains.

The best way to understand such protective strategies is as a combination of investing and insuring. Just as insurance costs money, downside protection is also achieved at the expense of reduced profit. In addition, these products can be bought with different levels of risk protection—much as your homeowners' insurance offers you widely varying deductible levels to choose from.

While option use is a common and effective tool for managing risk in institutional markets, there are still no integrated products that are simple, transparent, and cost-effective enough for mass retail application. In fact, some of the supposedly protective products that are being promoted to consumers today can be downright deceptive. Still, the situation may well improve. There is plenty of consumer interest, the tools exist, and the potential benefits are large. It's a trend to watch for.

Other types of vehicles that propose to deliver upside along with downside protection are also on their way to market. One of the more popular ones to emerge in recent years is the deferred variable annuity with a guaranteed lifetime withdrawal benefit, or GLWB.

This benefit guarantees a lifetime minimum withdrawal rate, usually available once the annuity has been held for a specified minimum amount of time. The initial premium is invested in mutual funds at the buyer's direction and held in subaccounts. No matter how the underlying investments perform, though, the withdrawal rate is guaranteed—even if the subaccounts' value declines all the way to zero. This insulation from market risk is a core attraction of the GLWB feature.

There are dozens of variations on this theme. Some insurance companies have products that allow the withdrawal rate to increase if you wait longer before you start taking money out. Others have graduated withdrawal rates tied to a full spectrum of age bands. And additional riders or benefits are available for a fee.

Buyers participate—to a limited extent—in market upside. One way they do so is in the control they typically retain over their money, a feature that in itself appeals to a broad audience of potential buyers. The subaccount value fluctuates with the market, so it stands to rise in value with good performance—but it's not insulated from downside risk either.

If the annuitant dies, the money that remains in the subaccount can be passed on to heirs. Death benefits are typically equal to the greater of the remaining cash value or the remaining premium less withdrawals and applicable surrender charges. This is where the market's performance during the holding period will leave its mark.

Another way the GLWBs capture upside is in the step-up feature that some issuers provide. These allow for the recalculation of account values at set intervals, such as every 5 or 10 years. If account values have risen beyond the level of the initial premium, then payouts can rise.

However, the annuity's fees eat significantly into this upside potential. These can be substantial—adding up to more than 3.5 or even 4 percent each year—and are deducted from the annuity's value each year. Generally speaking, the market would have to really boom for the subaccount value to rise much.

Still, it's worth remembering that the fees are purchasing a form of longevity insurance and death benefits along with a guaranteed annual payout.

It's wise to consult a trusted and knowledgeable advisor to navigate the complex features of the variable annuity's GLWB and related riders. An advisor can help you decide if it's a suitable product and feature for you, what the optimal benefits and fees for you might look like, and how to minimize commissions. In addition, there are complex legal and tax matters—such as who is the owner, who is the beneficiary, and so on—that can harm a surviving spouse's financial and tax situation if not done right.

The GWLB is an example of a minimum payment that is contractually guaranteed. The issuer has put it in writing. Offsetting the high value of the guarantee, though, are both its cost and potential questions about the underlying strength of the insurance company guarantor.

Take the guarantee out of the equation, and you'll find other products in development that also focus on providing a minimum payout to retirees along with upside exposure, but hinge instead on the good-faith pledge of a dependable manager. The promise to deliver, come hell or high water, is replaced by a pledged outcome that is highly likely but not certain.

In this category are several managed account solutions, currently in development or newly launched, that propose to deliver a minimum lifetime monthly income to their participants. These accounts are designed for employer retirement plans such as 401(k)s. In order to meet their monthly income bogeys, they plan to use the matching strategies that were once the sole province of traditional (defined benefit) pension plans.

In this approach, participants' minimum monthly income needs become the fund's dated liabilities, to be matched with corresponding assets to ensure success. Instead of emphasizing the vagaries of the glide path toward retirement, they focus on reaching their monthly income target safely. And by taking the basic income needs of their different participants into account, they are hoping to achieve mass customization without excessive cost.[2]

So there is good news on the horizon. Stay posted. And in the meantime, stay safe and keep your eye on your destinations. Risk less. And prosper.

Notes

Preface

1. Iyengar, Sheena. *The Art of Choosing*. New York, NY: Twelve. Hachette Book Group, 2010. The phenomenon Iyengar describes is called the "paradox of choice." See also Sethi-Iyengar, S., G. Huberman, and Jiang Wei. "How Much Choice is Too Much?" In *Pension Design and Structure: New Lessons from Behavioral Finance*, edited by Olivia S. Mitchell and Stephen P. Utkus, Chapter 5. New York: Oxford University Press, 2004.

Chapter 2: Picturing Your Destination

1. There are some good resources on the Web for identifying and analyzing your goals. See, in particular, www.goalgami.com/content/index.php. See also www.mint.com, for their modules dealing with goals.
2. For two short instructional videos that capture the distinction between needs and wants see www.youtube.com/watch?v=Mqzq03DiSVw and www.youtube.com/watch?v=tZFGoOQ20-g&feature=related.

Chapter 3: Paying Up

1. The Goalgami web site is a useful accompaniment to the material in this chapter as well as Chapter 2. See www.goalgami.com
2. Shefrin, H., and M. Statman. "Behavioral Portfolio Theory." *Journal of Financial and Quantitative Analysis* 35, no. 2 (June 2000): 127–151.

Chapter 4: The Mismeasure of Risk

1. Schaus, Stacy L. *Designing Successful Target-Date Strategies for Defined Contribution Plans: Putting Participants on the Optimal Glide Path.* New York: Wiley, 2010, p. 198.
2. Siegel, Jeremy J. *Stocks for the Long Run: The Definitive Guide to Financial Market Returns and Long Term Investment Strategies.* 4th ed. New York: McGraw-Hill, 2007. Siegel's book, which first appeared in 1994, makes the case that stocks are not very risky when held for a long time.
3. Samuelson, Paul A. "The Long-Term Case for Equities and How It Can Be Oversold," *Journal of Portfolio Management* 21, no.1 (Fall 1994): 15–24.
4. See the transcript of a debate between Zvi Bodie and Jeremy Siegel, "The Great Debate," The National Association of Personal Financial Advisors, NAPFA 2004 National Conference, Toronto, April 23, 2004. www.zvibodie.com/files/BodieSiegel_Debate_transcript.pdf
5. For an explicit and representative lesson on the supposedly inverse relationship between risk and time for all investors, we suggest you try this classic Java applet at www.smartmoney.com/personal-finance/retirement/time-vs-risk-7964.
6. The fallacies in the conventional wisdom about stocks persist in popular investment advice. See, for example, www.investopedia.com/articles/stocks/07/mistakes.asp?partner=basics8#axzz1UBinzwHa.

Chapter 5: The Allure of Hope

1. For the used-car salesman reference, see the *Stanford News*'s obituary for Amos Tverksy, *Stanford News Service*, 6/5/96, http://news.stanford.edu/pr/96/960605tversky.html.
2. The interview with Daniel Kahneman appears in Ackman, Dan, "Nobel Laureate Debunks Economic Theory." Forbes.com (November 6, 2002), www.forbes.com/2002/11/06/cx_da_1106nobel1.html.
3. Kahneman, D., and A. Tversky. "Prospect Theory: An Analysis of Decision under Risk." *Econometrica*, 47, no. 2, (March 1979): 263–291, www.princeton.edu/~kahneman/docs/Publications/prospect_theory.pdf.

4. Siegel, Jeremy J. *Stocks for the Long Run: The Definitive Guide to Financial Market Returns and Long Term Investment Strategies.* 4th ed. New York: McGraw-Hill, 2007.

5. Glassman, James K., and Kevin A.Hassett. *Dow 36,000: The New Strategy for Profiting from the Coming Rise in the Stock Market.* New York: Times Books, 1999.

6. Gould, Stephen Jay. "The Streak of Streaks." *The New York Review of Books* 35, no. 13, (August 18): 8–12, www.nybooks .com/articles/archives/1988/aug/18/the-streak-of-streaks.

7. Gilovich, T., R. Vallone, and A. Tversky. "The Hot Hand in Basketball: On the Misperception of Random Sequences." *Cognitive Psychology* 17 (1985): 295–314, www.psych.cornell.edu/ sec/pubPeople/tdg1/Gilo.Vallone.Tversky.pdf.

Chapter 6: Your Personal Risk Profile

1. See Bodie, Z., R. C. Merton, and W. F. Samuelson. "Labor Supply Flexibility and Portfolio Choice in a Life-Cycle Model." *Journal of Economic Dynamics and Control* 16 (1992): 427–449.

2. An excellent resource for risk profiling is *Finametrica,* where you can also find a good online risk tolerance assessment questionnaire: www.riskprofiling.com.

3. For more on bad psychological tests, see Davey, G., J. E Grable, and M. J. Roszkowski. "Insights from Psychology and Psychometrics on Measuring Risk Tolerance." *Journal of Financial Planning* (April 2005): 66–77, http://spwfe.fpanet.org:10005/ public/Unclassified%20Records/FPA%20Journal%20 April%202005%20-%20Insights%20from%20Psychology %20and%20Psychometrics%20on%20Measuring%20Risk%20 Tolerance.pdf. Geoff Davey is cofounder and director of *Finametrica.*

4. Davey, Geoff. "Assessing Risk Tolerance Scientifically." *Journal of Financial Planning* (September 2010) 23–25, www.risk profiling.com/Downloads/Assessing_RT_Scientifically.pdf.

Chapter 7: Finding the Safe Investment Zone

1. For news and information about TIPS, see the blog http:// explorebonds.com/, whose owner also continues to own the Financebuff blog http://thefinancebuff.com/. The Finance

Buff is also the author of *Explore TIPS: A Practical Guide to Investing in Treasury Inflation-Protected Securities* (CreateSpace, 2010). Another blog focused on TIPS that has recently launched is by journalist Dave Enna, who blogs at http://tipswatch.com.

2. Brett Arend. "Holding TIPS Will Make You Poorer." *MarketWatch* (May 6, 2011), http://www.marketwatch.com/story/tips-the-latest-big-steal-2011-05-06.

3. For a good introduction to TIPS and I Bonds, go to the TreasuryDirect web site, www.treasurydirect.gov/indiv/products/products.htm.

4. There is also a somewhat different table comparing I Bonds and TIPS on TreasuryDirect web site. www.treasurydirect.gov/indiv/products/prod_tipsvsibonds.htm.

5. Bob Hinkley has an impressive web site with a history of all TIPS coupons as well as index ratios for all TIPS outstanding: http://web.me.com/rlhinkley/tips/index.html.

Chapter 8: The Art of Matchmaking

1. Two funds backed by TIPS ladders are PIMCO Real Income TM 2019 Fund and PIMCO Real Income TM 2029 Fund. The TIPS in these portfolios are guaranteed by the U.S. government, but the funds' distributions are not guaranteed.

2. For an excellent introduction to annuities, see Pechter, Kerry. *Annuities for Dummies*. 3rd ed. New York: Wiley, 2008.

3. The Income Solutions web site is www.incomesolutions.com. There is also a good podcast interview of Kelli Hueler, founder and CEO of the Hueler Companies (developer of Income Solutions) at www.incomesolutions.com/Podcast.aspx.

4. For a good discussion of annuities, including an analysis of the role of default risk, see Babbel, David F. and Craig B. Merrill. "Rational Decumulation." Wharton Financial Institutions Working Paper #06-14, May 2007, http://fic.wharton.upenn.edu/fic/papers/06/0614.pdf.

5. A.M. Best's web site is www.ambest.com.

6. For more on state insurance guaranty agencies, see the web site of the National Organization of Life & Health Insurance Guaranty Associations, www.nolhga.com.

7. One web site with very good tools and calculators is newretirement.com. (Co-author Zvi Bodie is on the advisory board.)

Chapter 9: Investing Safely for Education

1. Many web sites offer help in navigating financial aid and education financing. Some good places to begin are: http://nces .ed.gov/collegenavigator, http://studentaid.ed.gov, and www .savingforcollege.com.
2. See IRS Publication 970. *Tax Benefits for Education*. www.irs .gov/pub/irs-pdf/p970.pdf.
3. See www.privatecollege529.com.
4. To help you compare different 529 plans, the web site www .savingforcollege.com offers a premium monthly membership (for a monthly subscription fee), which is worth considering.

Chapter 10: Choosing Risky Investments

1. Index funds may be more reliable especially in more developed markets such as U.S. large company stocks. For more on the poor record of actively managed funds in comparison with passive index funds, once expenses are taken into account, see Fama, Eugene F. and Kenneth R. French. "Luck versus Skill in the Cross-Section of Mutual Fund Returns." *Journal of Finance* 65, no. 5: 1915–1947.
2. For more on your home as an investment, see Bodie, Zvi and M. Clowes. *Worry-Free Investing*. Upper Saddle River, NJ: Financial Times/Prentice Hall, 2003, Chapter 5.
3. Vanguard's passive REIT index fund has a low expense ratio. See https://personal.vanguard.com/us/FundsSnapshot?Fund Id=0123&FundIntExt=INT.
4. Since 2003, qualified dividends have also been taxed at a lower rate (not more than 15%). The tax law on which this favorable treatment is based expires at the end of 2012, so dividend taxation may change.

Chapter 11: How to Choose an Advisor

1. A few good places to start your search for an advisor are http://findanadvisor.napfa.org, www.fpanet.org, and www.cfp .net/search. The CFA Institute also provides good guidance at www.cfainstitute.org/about/investor/Pages/index.aspx.

2. Other professional societies that have searchable directories of financial advisors include the Personal Financial Planning Division of the American Institute of Certified Public Accountants, at www.aicpa.org/INTERESTAREAS/PERSONALFINANCIALPLANNING/Pages/default.aspx, and the Society of Financial Service Professionals at www.financialpro.org. (We suggest that you start with NAPFA or FPA or CFP.net, however.)

3. William Sharpe's hilarious video, "The Wrong Financial Advisor" is *de rigueur* before hiring a financial advisor. Find it on our companion web site or on YouTube, www.youtube.com/watch?v=Vv4HQG2Hz0I.

4. See Smetters, Kent. "Finding an Honest Financial Advisor," *Legalzoom* (April 2011), www.legalzoom.com/money-matters/personal-finance/finding-honest-financial-advisor. Kent Smetters is the founder of Veritat Advisors, a Web-based financial advisory service for smaller investors, with affordable fees. Coauthor Zvi Bodie is a member of Veritat's Board of Advisors.

5. See also the advice of seasoned financial planner and FPA Board member Paula Hogan, who has a crisp checklist on her web site, www.paulahogan.com.

6. See Ellis, C. "The Winners' Game." *Financial Analysts Journal* 67, no. 4 (July-August 2011).

7. For due diligence and more about ADV forms, see the SEC web site at www.adviserinfo.sec.gov and www.sec.gov/answers/formadv.htm. For ADV forms of brokers, see www.finra.org/Investors/ToolsCalculators/BrokerCheck .

8 For broker-dealer disciplinary histories, see www.nasaa.org/home/index.cfm. For the CFP Board of Standards, see www.CFP.net.

9. For further reading, see the Certified Financial Planner Board of Standards, "Questions to Ask When Choosing a Planner," www.letsmakeaplan.org/ux/pdf/10_Questions.pdf. See also Kirchner, Bonnie. *Who Can You Trust with Your Money?* Upper Saddle River, NJ: FT Press, 2010. For an excellent interview of Kirchner, see www.wgbh.org/programs/Greater-Boston-11/episodes/Apr-21-2010Bonnie-Kirchners-Who-Can-You-Trust-With-Your-Money-14906. For more on how to spot investment scams, see www.youtube.com/watch?v=mABf0LN9Jus&feature=youtu.be.

Epilogue

1. Influential proponents of the "safety-first" approach include FPA Board member Paula Hogan (www.paulahogan.com) and François Gadenne, founder of the Retirement Income Industry Association. See Gadenne, François and Mike Zwecher. *Body of Knowledge for RIIA's Retirement Management Analyst* ^{SM} *(RMA*^{SM}*)Designation: How to Benefit from the "View Across the Silos": From Investment Management to Retirement Income and Retirement Management.* Boston, MA: RIIA Publishing, 2009–2011.

2. Among the managed account solutions discussed are Dimensional Managed DC, from Dimensional Fund Advisors, and Income Plus from Financial Engines.

About the Authors

Zvi Bodie is the Norman and Adele Barron Professor of Management at Boston University. He holds a Ph.D. from the Massachusetts Institute of Technology and has served on the finance faculty at the Harvard Business School and MIT's Sloan School of Management.

Zvi has published widely on pension finance and investment strategy in leading professional journals. His books include *The Future of Life Cycle Saving and Investing* and *Foundations of Pension Finance*. His textbook, *Investments*, coauthored by Alex Kane and Alan Marcus, is the market leader and is used in the certification programs of the CFA Institute and the Society of Actuaries. His textbook, *Financial Economics*, is coauthored by Nobel Prize–winning economist Robert C. Merton. Zvi is also coauthor of *Worry Free Investing: A Safe Approach to Achieving Your Lifetime Financial Goals*.

In 2007 the Retirement Income Industry Association gave him their Lifetime Achievement in Applied Retirement Research Award. Zvi's web site is zvibodie.com.

Rachelle Taqqu is a financial services professional and former banker. She holds the CFA designation and has advised individuals, corporations, and nonprofits on a wide variety of investments and strategic decisions.

Rachelle earned an Honors BA from the University of Toronto, a Ph.D. with Distinction from Columbia University, and an MBA with Distinction from Cornell University. She is the coauthor or editor of two books and several articles about aspects of economic history and economic development.

Index